BASIC TEXTS IN COUNSELLING AND PSYCHOTHERAPY

Series editors: Arlene Vetere and Rudi Dallos

This series introduces readers to the theory and practice of counselling and psychotherapy across a wide range of topic areas. The books appeal to anyone wishing to use counselling and psychotherapeutic skills and are particularly relevant to workers in health, education, social work and related settings. The books are unusual in being rooted in psychodynamic and systemic ideas, yet being written at an accessible, readable and introductory level. Each text offers theoretical background and guidance for practice, with creative use of clinical examples.

Published

Jenny Altschuler
COUNSELLING AND PSYCHOTHERAPY FOR FAMILIES IN TIMES OF ILLNESS AND DEATH 2nd Edition

Bill Barnes, Sheila Ernst and Keith Hyde
AN INTRODUCTION TO GROUPWORK

Stephen Briggs
WORKING WITH ADOLESCENTS AND YOUNG ADULTS 2nd Edition

Alex Coren
SHORT-TERM PSYCHOTHERAPY 2nd Edition

Jim Crawley and Jan Grant
COUPLE THERAPY

Emilia Dowling and Gill Gorell Barnes
WORKING WITH CHILDREN AND PARENTS THROUGH SEPARATION AND DIVORCE

Loretta Franklin
AN INTRODUCTION TO WORKPLACE COUNSELLING

Gill Gorell Barnes
FAMILY THERAPY IN CHANGING TIMES 2nd Edition

Fran Hedges
AN INTRODUCTION TO SYSTEMATIC THERAPY WITH INDIVIDUALS

Fran Hedges
REFLEXIVITY IN THERAPEUTIC PRACTICE

Margaret Henning
POSITIVE DYNAMICS

John Hills
INTRODUCTION TO SYSTEMIC AND FAMILY THERAPY

Sally Hodges
COUNSELLING ADULTS WITH LEARNING DISABILITIES

Linda Hopper
COUNSELLING AND PSYCHOTHERAPY WITH CHILDREN AND ADOLESCENTS

Sue Kegerreis
PSYCHODYNAMIC COUNSELLING WITH CHILDREN AND YOUNG PEOPLE

continued overleaf...

Geraldine Shipton
WORKING WITH EATING DISORDERS

Gerrilyn Smith
WORKING WITH TRAUMA

Laurence Spurling
AN INTRODUCTION TO PSYCHODYNAMIC COUNSELLING 2nd Edition

Paul Terry
COUNSELLING AND PSYCHOTHERAPY WITH OLDER PEOPLE 2nd Edition

Jan Wiener and Mannie Sher
COUNSELLING AND PSYCHOTHERAPY IN PRIMARY HEALTH CARE

Shula Wilson
DISABILITY, COUNSELLING AND PSYCHOTHERAPY

Steven Walker
CULTURALLY COMPETENT THERAPY

Jenny Walters
WORKING WITH FATHERS

Jessica Yakeley
WORKING WITH VIOLENCE

Invitation to authors
The Series Editors welcome proposals for new books within the Basic Texts in Counselling and Psychotherapy series. These should be sent to Arlene Vetere at the University of Surrey (email a.vetere@surrey.ac.uk) or Rudi Dallos at Plymouth University (email R.Dallos@plymouth.ac.uk)

Basic Texts in Counselling and Psychotherapy
Series Standing Order ISBN 978–0–333–69330–8
(outside North America only)

You can receive future titles in this series as they are published by placing a standing order. Please contact your bookseller or, in the case of difficulty, write to us at the address below with your name and address, the title of the series and the ISBN quoted above. Customer Services Department, Macmillan Distribution Ltd Houndmills, Basingstoke, Hampshire RG21 6XS, England

POSITIVE DYNAMICS

A Systemic Narrative Approach to Facilitating Groups

MARGARET HENNING

First published 2016
by PALGRAVE

Palgrave in the UK is an imprint of Macmillan Publishers Limited, registered in England, company number 785998, of 4 Crinan Street, London, N1 9XW.

Palgrave Macmillan in the US is a division of St Martin's Press LLC, 175 Fifth Avenue, New York, NY 10010.

Palgrave is a global imprint of the above companies and is represented throughout the world.

Palgrave® and Macmillan® are registered trademarks in the United States, the United Kingdom, Europe and other countries.

ISBN 978-1-137-43056-4   ISBN 978-1-137-43057-1 (eBook)

DOI 10.1007/978-1-137-43057-1

A catalogue record for this book is available from the British Library.

A catalog record for this book is available from the Library of Congress.

CONTENTS

List of Figures, Genograms and Tables   viii

1 Groups and Social Realities   **1**
Why this book?   1
Meet the author   5
The need for a new theory base   6
Some definitions   7
The primacy of relationship and necessity of groups   9
Conflict   11
Different types of groups   13
The dimension of function   16
The dimension of theory base   17
The dimension of leadership style   18
Evaluating the group   21
Summary: why this book, and how is it structured?   22

**2 Basics of Systemic Thinking and Groups as an Ecology
of Minds**   **24**
Thinking systemically   24
Relationships, process and circular causality   29
Multiple generations: process patterns through time   33
Group work and the group as an ecology of minds   34
Attachment styles and group process   35
Using genograms, eco maps and other diagrams   39
Sculpts and action methods   43
Summary: groups as social systems and ecologies of minds   45

**3 Narrative Theory and Some Basics of Human
Communication for Optimal Group Dynamics**   **47**
Social constructionism   47
Life as story: deconstructing the problem plot and
co-creating the preferred outcome   50

The narrative critique		51
Exceptions and the 'flip side'		53
Scaffolding, content and kinds of question		54
Radical listening and deconstructing		56
Externalising		58
Landscaping and values		60
Re-membering, re-telling and outsider witnessing		66
Writings and ceremonies		67
Summary: the essence of a narrative approach		69
4	**Group Development over Time: Setting the Culture and Deepening Engagement**	**70**
	Preparing to start a group	70
	The emotional shape of a session	76
	Which emotions?	79
	The developmental stage of a group	80
	Starting a group: setting the culture	81
	Bouncing the ball: nuances of engagement	83
	Silences and mindfulness	85
	The 'what are you all thinking?' round	86
	Starting with a group which has been ongoing before the facilitator joins	88
	The open group: when new members join	90
	The group review	90
	Summary	92
5	**Specific Process Issues**	**93**
	Good and bad conformity	93
	Power	96
	Commenting on process and dropping hypotheses on the floor	98
	Healthy communication	99
	Conflict with, or attack directed at, the facilitator	100
	Dealing with dyadic conflict	102
	The person who talks too much	105
	Aggression, passive-aggression and assertiveness	106
	Summary	111
6	**Putting It All Together: Some Sample Applications**	**112**
	The family consultation model	112
	The supervision group review	114

CONTENTS

The training course for carers of people with serious
mental health problems   119
The mental health inpatient ward open patients' group   123
The organisational team debrief after serious
untoward incidents   133
Last words   137

References and Bibliography   139
Index   142

LIST OF FIGURES, GENOGRAMS AND TABLES

Figure 2.1 Interaction between Joe's systems   24
Figure 2.2 Basic systemic concepts   25
Figure 3.1 Landscaping   61
Figure 4.1 Emotional intensity of Martha's session   77
Figure 4.2 Emotional intensity of a usual session   78
Figure 4.3 Emotional intensity of Keith's session   79
Figure 5.1 Symmetrical and complementary escalation   101
Figure 5.2 Points at which to deal with anger response   108

Genogram 2.1 Bev team eco map   40
Genogram 2.2 Bev genogram   41

Table 3.1 Mapping the problem in externalising   59

GROUPS AND SOCIAL REALITIES

Why this book?

Jill is sitting in her course Personal Development Group and hating it as usual. Maggie and James have already started squabbling about gender and power. They always take up much of the talking time and at this point of the academic year Jill is beginning to feel desperate because she knows that their participation will be noted and yet she has said nothing at all to date. Jean, the facilitator, is sitting silently, as she nearly always does, but Jill is sure she is watching her and realising her inadequacies. She feels that these will be fed back to the course staff group even though this is theoretically a 'safe space'.

Maggie is getting to the point where she wants to shriek out obscenities. She is bitterly angry that this group seems to use her as a scapegoat and allocate to her the role of 'bossy bitch'. She is supposed to be learning to 'self-reflect' but her emotional arousal is such that she can't reflect on anything but blaming others for her situation. Today she had promised herself that she would remain silent but James and Lisa had immediately started needling her until she lashed out verbally.

GROUP 1

The above scenario is still unfortunately familiar to group participants in the field of therapies and psychology, whether in development or training groups or in group therapy. The task of the facilitator is defined as noting and possibly interpreting the interactive dynamics which arise spontaneously. In theory terms, the facilitator will 'discover' real, neurotic aspects of the participants' psychic functioning or of the whole group's psychic functioning (see, for example, Bion 1961, Foulkes & Anthony 1957). To what extent this functioning has been induced by characteristics of the total relational space is not sufficiently taken into account. In high threat situations, we all become more rigid and defensive and learning and creativity are seriously compromised.

Carl Rogers, whose ideas about groups were very influential in the **encounter groups** period, came from the opposite direction. He believed that man is basically good, with an actualising tendency, and that therefore the group could be trusted to run itself. Thorne and Sanders (2013, p. 14) remark that *'he believed in the capacity of the group to find its own way forward and by refusing to exert his authority in the normal way he helped establish a truly democratic climate in which power-sharing became a daily reality'*. This commitment to democratic process opened up very important advances in theorising about therapeutic groups and education but this opposite direction still produced a group in which there was insufficient control over dynamics, leading to problems.

In business groups (e.g. team meetings, strategy meetings, focus groups) there is usually a fixed agenda and a task focus. This means that group dynamics are not generally observed or theorised by the group leader and often do not seem to intrude too obviously on the achievement of the task. Relational space tends to be kept more positive by a strong task focus. In fact, organisational and business group development has usually asked the question, 'How do we get the objectives met in as timely and efficient way as possible?'

So, is the whole secret of running successful groups to keep a strong task focus? It certainly can be useful and positive to do so. However, the lack of attention to interpersonal dynamics can seriously undermine the attainment of task. Leaders running this type of group often find the group process is ambushed by negative interactions. There is no option but to see this as accidental and possibly to blame, or even exclude, particular individuals.

Many therapeutic and training groups also have a strong task focus. For example, **Cognitive Behaviour Therapy (CBT)** groups work through the individual group member's interaction with the (instructional) material. Other group members supply a social (and hopefully supportive) context but the relational dynamics are not seen as needing to be theorised as part of the therapeutic endeavour. Some theorists would say that this might not, therefore, be a true group but rather an **aggregate** (defined as individuals sharing a space, such as a classroom, but not necessarily relating with each other). I would argue that learning is enhanced and task effectiveness is increased in a positive and cohesive group environment.

So there we have the two contrasting valences of the current ways of doing group work; attend to dynamics or attend to task. Of course,

I am simplifying for the sake of clarity. Even with a strong task focus the leader might well be paying some attention to dynamics and even in a group therapy or personal development situation there may be attention to tasks.

I believe that whatever the type of group, the facilitator should be noting and working with **both task focus and relational dynamics**, with a duty of intervening proactively to **keep relational space optimised for the achievement of task and the benefit of participants**. In some longer-term groups, such as work teams, the necessity for a joint focus becomes even more obviously essential. In natural, relatively permanent groups, such as the family or nation, there are leadership roles but little formal allocation of the duty of facilitation.

What can a group member do if the leader or facilitator does not facilitate? Actually, any member can take some responsibility for group dynamics in a relatively unstructured situation. Let us use the above example and see what can change.

Maggie discusses the difficulties of the group in her individual supervision and her supervisor suggests that she should take responsibility herself for making the dynamics less dysfunctional. She decides to try a version of the **miracle question** *(De Shazar & Dolan 2007). Accordingly, she comments early in the next group meeting, 'I wonder what we will see happening in this group if a miracle has happened overnight and the group is meeting each of our needs in a really satisfying way?' After a short pause, people start addressing themselves to this question and the conversation becomes much more positive than it has been before.*

Jill still lacks the confidence to join in but Maggie has noticed her silence and at a point in the ensuing conversation turns to her and asks, 'Jill, I wonder what you are thinking about that?' Jill replies with what she is thinking and finds to her surprise that her ideas are well received in the group. This makes it easier for her to take part in future discussions.

GROUP 1

When the meeting is very structured, it is less possible for a member to step into this facilitator position. The chair is in charge. The group member usually has the right to suggest agenda items. There might be limited opportunities to apply some of the techniques described later; however, this book is written primarily for those who have the task of leading or facilitating any groups, whether business meetings, teams, therapy or supervision groups, teaching or training, or any other.

What about groups which by definition have 'no facilitator'? There are some groups which are defined by their nature as egalitarian and

3

leaderless. An example of this would be a peer support or peer supervision group. As we see in the Group 1 example, a member could unilaterally take up the role. This could give rise to some problem dynamics. If the unofficial facilitator has a high enough comparative status the group can accept this and it can work but then there actually is a de facto leader. Maggie, in the above example, will almost certainly generate resentment in one or more of the others in the room and one would hope that this potential cost was thoroughly explored in her supervision before she took the step.

If this leaderless group wishes to remain such it is necessary to agree at inception what arrangements can be made for someone to facilitate; to take responsibility for dynamics and task structuring. It might be decided that all should take responsibility but this rarely works out without some social awkwardness and the risk of splitting and/or loss of impetus. The group as a whole can easily become inefficient in any or all of its functions. There are possible solutions. For example there can be a rolling programme of a different member taking up the role in each separate meeting and it might even be decided to allocate facilitation and structuring to different individuals in any given meeting.

This book therefore aims to be a practical manual for group **facilitators**, whether therapists, supervisors, managers, educators or even members who are taking up the role. Grounded in a firm psychological evidence base, it focuses on the concrete practicalities of how to make groups vehicles for success, whether in achieving therapy or self-development, in optimising team functioning or in achieving specific organisational tasks. The general theory and technique are covered first and some specific applications are later described.

FOR REFLECTION

- Think of a group you belong to. How much are you aware of the task/s and how much of the dynamics or relationships?
- Now do the same reflection with another group you belong to. Is the task/dynamics balance the same or different? Why?
- Who facilitates each of these? Is the facilitator also the group leader?
- Who holds what power in these groups? Why that person or those people?
- What would you or wouldn't you say in that group? Why?

Meet the author

Before we start, you might want to know a little about who is writing this book and why. I am a Consultant Clinical Psychologist and Family (Systemic) Psychotherapist with a background in teaching, especially the teaching of adults and children with specific learning disabilities or emotional difficulties.

Since leaving teaching and re-training in psychology and family therapy, I have been engaged in various forms of group facilitation for about 25 years. Starting with therapeutic work with traditional extended families in Zimbabwe, I also facilitated family therapy teams and engaged in interactive training and in team development for various organisations. Coming to the UK in 1997, I worked for the NHS, where I was soon involved in management but also continued to engage in training, therapy, supervision and team building, refining and developing the model explained in this book.

I currently have a private practice, which includes all of the same activities. Apart from being a therapist, I do some training and university teaching and continue to offer group and team supervision, both in the NHS and the Voluntary Sector.

I am a committed Christian, a widow with a 'tribe' of children, grandchildren and great-grandchildren. As a white person from Africa I have always had to grapple with ideas about cultural difference and relative power. When I worked in Harare Central Hospital with (usually poor, rural, traditional) black Zimbabweans, I developed my reliance on client families' **alternative knowledges** (see Chapter 3) as I was dependent on client families for instruction on cultural issues. Because my own behaviour might be culturally inappropriate, I had to ask explicitly for the client's input on whether this was so, and on the fit between their requirements and my responses (Henning 1992). I had to become curious about how to flatten the power hierarchy in order for them to be willing to be frank with me; the interactive and cultural issues of what is not communicated and why.

As a child I was considered odd and was always on the periphery of any group, watching the interactions. I was, and have continued to be, deeply curious about the interplay of the internal representations of individuals with their behaviours in the social group, whether culture, family or peer group. Often a rebel, I developed an interest in why different people think differently and why consensus is reached, sometimes with a false conclusion. Above all, I noted how the group could nurture or destroy people, how necessary tasks could be achieved optimally or fatally hindered by the emotions and actions of group members. Not surprisingly, therefore, I am passionate about the positive effects of attending to group dynamics in any group context and deliberately generating optimal conditions for groups to achieve their functions.

FOR REFLECTION

- Why are you reading this book? How do you hope it might be useful to you?
- How have you related to various groups in your own life?
- Have you noticed groups being constructive or destructive? Why did they have those effects?

The need for a new theory base

Much of Social Psychology has been about the study of groups. Indeed, this area of psychological research and theorising is about people in interaction with other people, whether at the level of a small group or a culture. Sometimes this body of knowledge has been largely ignored by small group theorists. Their thinking about how groups work has come from two directions: theories of individual functioning (and pathology) and theories of task achievement. Generally speaking the latter has been more espoused in management and business and the former in psychotherapy.

Most training of group therapists, in spite of this wide body of research in the field of Social Psychology, is based on old, untested ideas of 'group dynamics'. Discovering the rage and 'shadow side' of insecurities and hostilities, which frequently emerged in unstructured and effectively un-facilitated groups (as in *Group 1* above), theorists assumed that they were uncovering what was inevitably there and that it was necessary to allow the transference, basic assumption groups or group tension to reveal themselves and play themselves out (Whitely & Gordon 1979). Yalom and Leszcz (2005) and others critiqued some of the difficulties and pointed out that the main usefulness of group work arose from **mutual support** but still the focus of group work was around problematic rather than positive interactions. In terms of **Narrative** theory (Chapter 3), they were simply co-creating a negative and noxious story and process. Far from this 'uncovering' being therapeutic, **Systemic Narrative** therapists would consider it a social construction which is anti-therapeutic, creating iatrogenic psychological damage to the individuals and the group.

Unfortunately, there is little in the literature to date which reflects this radically different way of looking at the therapeutic potential of groups. This book aims to meet this need by linking theory with the extensive experience of the author in running groups of various purposes.

In management there are fewer 'negative stories' about group dynamics and groups are often task-focused, which in itself makes the process more easily functional and positive. However, managers may not realise that the pattern of relationships in the group is their business. They may not know that the task could be even better achieved if, for example, the creative potential of each individual were deliberately supported and defensiveness relating to change processes or power hierarchies were minimised.

So, there is a considerable Social Psychology literature about group processes. **Systemic** approaches (see Chapter 2) and interpersonal ideas derived from **Social Constructionism** (see Chapter 3) add ideas from psychotherapeutic clinical practice to this experimental literature. As a Consultant Clinical Psychologist and Family Psychotherapist, my own preferred orientation is **Systemic Narrative**, a combination of basic **Family (Systemic) Therapy** and **Narrative (Social Constructionist)** ideas.

Strangely, although these approaches deal explicitly with people in relationship, there is very little focus on groups per se in Systemic or Narrative literature. The former focuses largely on the family and the latter on the individual, even though this is the individual in relational space. This book aims to be a tool in bridging that gap.

Some definitions

What is a **group**? The Chambers Dictionary defines it as, *'a number of individual things or people related in some definite way differentiating them from others'*. In this book, of course, we are not interesting ourselves in the things which make up groups, only in groups of people.

Brown (2000, p. 4) summarises, *'a great many groups can be characterized as a collection of people bound together by some common experience or purpose, or who are interrelated in a micro-social structure, or who interact with one another'*, and adds, *'perhaps the crucial necessary condition is that those same people also share some conception of themselves as belonging to the same social unit'*. He also points out the necessity that they are defined as such by at least one person outside the group.

We will not be considering groups in their widest definition because by definition these groups are not facilitated; we will look only at people, *'who are interrelated in a micro-social structure'*. Such a structure is a net of relationships with all its complexities. We will encounter status and hierarchy, roles, alliances, conformity and conflict, impact on individual identity, achievement or hindrance of tasks. These micro-social structures might well operate without a **facilitator** or even without any obvious **leader**, although careful examinations will show that most groups have an individual or individuals who take a lead.

A group **leader** is exactly that; someone who takes precedence in the group with a commensurate responsibility for achieving group tasks or functions. Sometimes there might be more than one leader (for example, the parents in a nuclear family, the elders in a church). This could be advantageous in supplying mutual support, if the leaders are able to collaborate effectively. On the other hand, leadership competition or conflict might make the group less functional or even destroy it completely.

A **facilitator** is someone who has the function of improving or making easier the functioning of the group and might not be the group leader, although the terms could sometimes be seen as interchangeable. In the example of Group 1 above, the leader, who should have been the facilitator, was not acting as such. Maggie decided to allocate that function to herself and was successful in so doing, although probably not as successful as the leader might have been. All else being equal, the higher the status of the facilitator the more facilitative power is available.

On the whole we will assume in this book that the leader is also the facilitator and will be addressing leaders, whether therapists, supervisors, managers, trainers, teachers or any other with responsibilities for how a group functions. Nevertheless, that responsibility does not reside only in the leadership. Group members should also be willing to facilitate in so far as they are able and should all take individual responsibility for successful interactions and task focus.

Group cohesion is a term frequently used by social psychologists and other group theorists. As a concept it includes how strongly members identify with the group, how salient that membership is in their self-concept and how much they are inclined to take on the attitudes and opinions of the group as a whole. Generally it is considered that strong group cohesion is desirable and positive in achievement of its functions, though there are some exceptions to this, which will be considered later (see Chapter 4).

Finally, what is the **function** of a group? We should probably speak of functions rather than function. I believe that every group should enhance the well-being and positive identity development of its members. It should optimise relationships, especially as these relate to the tasks of the group. More salient for most groups (though not necessarily more important) is the achievement of one or more tasks. These tasks might be individual for the members, as in learning or training groups. Alternatively they may be group or organisational tasks, as in focus groups, work departments, sports teams. The family is an example of a natural group with many functions, including emotional support, physical and financial protection, education and acculturation.

The primacy of relationship and necessity of groups

As I write this, a stand-up comedian is being interviewed on TV. He speaks of how important it is for the audience to become a group and how this is easier for the performer to engender in the provinces than in London, where the audience is more diverse. Group-ness is harder, but potentially richer, where there is diversity.

Groups are ubiquitous. We often label ourselves 'social animals' and indeed, people cannot live without other people. Our babies are totally dependent on others for their very lives, and as we grow that dependency becomes interdependency. The story of Robinson Crusoe fascinates us because of our uneasy sense that it is difficult or even impossible to live without others; no wonder that Defoe has to produce a Man Friday. In the Christian worldview the group and relationship predate the universe. Buddhists and Hindus see everything in the universe as being interrelated.

The modern world has depersonalised some of this dependency because so many of the necessities of life are produced by a much wider and personally unknown group. My food comes from all over the world and can be purchased at my local supermarket; I need not know the farmer. My rubbish is collected by the council. Heat and water are supplied without my having to interact with any particular individuals. I can forget my dependency on the myriads of other people who are necessary for supplying me with these means of living. There is a consequent possibility of comparative isolation and we recognise this as a problem. As we become more socially isolated our instinct to relate to others finds different ways to form groupings; the explosion of social media on the internet reflects this. The village has become worldwide. Sometimes these internet groups are described as 'virtual' but there is nothing virtual about them. They are real groups with the same power to influence members, the same possibilities of good or bad relationship processes, the same issues of who does or does not belong.

Sarah wakes in the morning and immediately becomes embroiled in the operation of her most primary group; her nuclear family. She has breakfast with her husband, organises the children and gets them off to school. She then has a few minutes to catch up on emails and internet social media, where she interacts in several other groups; her extended family, friends, special interest chat rooms. She goes to work, where the first item of the day is a team meeting – yet another group. After work she goes to choir practice – another group. Her whole day is spent in various groups.

Sarah's sense of her own identity is formed reciprocally in her groups. She might feel very secure or insecure depending on what input she is receiving about herself from her family or from her peer group. One level of status is a reflection of the group's status. She might see herself as a mediocre vocalist because her choir is not well-regarded (**between-group difference**); in the same way a footballer is labelled by the ratings of his team, an employee by the prestige of his firm. On the other hand she might see herself as a mediocre vocalist in a well-regarded choir if her fellow members are more talented or skilled than she is (**within-group difference**). Both dimensions might also, of course, make her believe herself an extremely talented vocalist. The footballer might be the star of his team, the employee the rising light in his firm. We define ourselves through both between-group and within-group differences.

FOR REFLECTION

- Choose a day in your last week and scan it from morning to night. What groups were you involved in during that day?
- How did each of those groups make you define yourself?
- Were you most influenced by within-group or between-group differences in each case?
- What other factors were involved in how you saw your identity in each of those groups?

Between-group dynamics are not the focus of this book but a little reflection will show how important they are. Wars and disregard for human rights arise from the stereotyping of other nations, cultures, classes, even gender. As soon as there is a 'we' and 'they' there is a possibility of demonising those we see as not grouped with us. One way to retain a sense of secure group membership is by deflecting conversations into complaints about 'the enemy without'. Group **cohesion** can be improved by an increase in between-group conflict, but at what cost?

In Sarah's work team there is huge dissatisfaction with the organisation's management. Team members complain to each other about the unfair demands being placed upon them. This helps them to feel close to each other, united against a common enemy. However, as the 'story' of the unfair management grows they also define their own team more and more as powerless and abused. Organisational tasks are undermined. Their perceived lack of team agency feeds a personal sense of lack of agency and they become more and more stressed and resentful. Sarah might well find that she becomes ill because of the anxiety and anger engendered.

Note that the 'story' might be founded on truth (more about this in Chapter 3). Nevertheless, between-group escalating dissatisfaction is not a solution. This is one example of where strong group cohesiveness has been gained at too high a price. Clear communication and between-group shared vision and collaboration are necessary (Brown 2000). This communication might not happen if the team feels sufficiently disempowered. In some ways the principles of between-group dynamics are similar to those within groups. For example, a group member who feels disempowered is unlikely to contribute actively. Brown considers between-group issues in some detail and his later research has been in this area. As stated before, it is not a particular focus of this book.

So, people live, work and develop themselves and their organisations in groups. Unfortunately, especially in times of stress or rapid change, or if negative stories arise about themselves or others, the patterns of relating either in or between groups can be noxious. People can become guarded and defensive, withholding their opinions, to the detriment of creativity and self-development. At worst there can be unspoken hostilities and rage, which lead to subtle undermining of the task, other groups or other group members. These negative emotions are, in turn, destructive to the individuals who are experiencing them.

Conflict

Conflict is defined by Chambers Dictionary as, *'unfortunate coincidence or opposition; violent collision; struggle, contest, war, etc; … to fight, to contend; to be in opposition; to clash'.* The general sense, in my mind, includes flavours of hostility, anxiety and aggression. Facilitators, whether in or between groups, have to have tools for reducing conflict and hostility while maintaining plenty of space for different points of view. Chapters 4 and 5 have sections dealing specifically with the management of conflict and potential conflict.

It is usually said that conflict is an essential part of group process. For example, Yalom and Leszcz (2005, p. 364) state, *'Some groups become "too nice" and diligently avoid conflict and confrontation, often mirroring the therapist's avoidance of aggression. Yet conflict is so inevitable in the course of a group's development that its absence suggests some impairment of the developmental sequence.'* My belief is that, although it might well arise, it is neither essential nor desirable, though it is true that the facilitator should not be avoidant and should be willing to deal proactively with whatever arises in the group, including conflict. These authors go on to say, *'Learning how to deal effectively with conflict is an important therapeutic step that contributes to individual maturation and emotional resilience.'* Yes. I consider that group facilitators and members should try to resolve conflict as soon as it appears, and in Chapters 4 and 5 I give the subject extensive consideration. I see no reason why one should not learn tools for dealing with conflict before the conflict occurs!

Some writers differentiate between dysfunctional and functional conflict. The differentiation seems to be that functional conflict is that which is resolved and dysfunctional that which is not resolved! Well, yes. The semantic problem in defining this way is that facilitators, in believing that conflict might be functional, might subliminally create a context in which it **becomes** inevitable. We know that states of high arousal (like Maggie's and even Jill's in Group 1 at the start of this chapter), far from improving our development or involvement with others, seriously hinder them. It is part of the facilitator's task to help keep any hostility or anxiety at a low enough level for engagement and creativity not to be hampered. This is the very opposite of what some group work practitioners do. Ruptures of relationship might happen (again, not inevitably) and it can be very good for group members to **learn how to heal them**. (If they cannot be healed there will be permanent damage to the group's functioning, unless one of the parties leaves the group.) I would argue, however, that they should never be engendered either deliberately or by a **dysfunctional story** (see Chapter 3) about their inevitability.

If by conflict what is meant is **disagreement**, that is a different matter. In a healthy group people can disagree with each other, can even be passionate about presenting their own points of view, but there must be a mechanism for respecting the other perspective and reaching solutions which are acceptable to all. Group theorists might well call this functional (as opposed to dysfunctional) conflict. I prefer to keep the issues clear by using the term disagreement. If group members can learn to disagree without hostility there might never be any conflict to resolve.

I would also argue that confrontation is not the same as conflict. Learning to confront others lovingly and gently is one of those skills which relate to individual maturation and emotional resilience. Congruence and transparency about one's own views should grow alongside respect for and openness to the views of others. Much of my own theorising has been about what constitutes healthy communication and I become more and more convinced that it should be as clear, complete and acknowledging of emotional reactions as possible.

FOR REFLECTION

- Think of some situations in which it feels comfortable to disagree with someone. What makes these situations safe?
- When do you feel you have to hide or suppress what you think and feel? Why?
- Think of the last time you confronted someone about something. Could you do it without conflict or did you need the impetus of anger and hostility?
- If confrontation felt difficult or had to be hostile, apply some of your answers to the first point and think about whether it could have been easier.

Different types of groups

On what dimensions do groups differ?

In the first place we might consider whether they are naturally occurring groups or whether they have been deliberately constructed.

Natural groups 'just happen'. They can be considered groups because people can define themselves as members or not. Am I a Christian or a Muslim? Am I British or French? Am I a man or a woman? Am I a doctor or a dancer? Am I a member of a profession? A trade union? A political party? A particular tribe or clan? A certain social group? A particular family? There may or may not be identified leaders in these naturally occurring groups and the facilitative role might be lodged in particular people, might be diffuse, might be missing. Usually leadership and facilitation is still necessary. Seen as social networks they might be very large and loose indeed or very small and tight. Usually we don't even think of them as groups. On the whole they are not the subject of our focus in this book.

Constructed groups are deliberately set up for a purpose. These might include certain social groups, for example a Morris dancing group, a choir, a photography club. Business or service organisations and teams are formed to achieve certain objectives. Also included here are learning/training groups, supervision and therapy groups. In constructed groups there are usually formal leadership positions (chairman, trainer, etc.) and facilitation becomes a clearer necessary function. Actually, the principles used in leading and facilitating a constructed group can also be used to promote positivity in permanent, natural groups. Although this book deals more specifically with the constructed group, readers should find that techniques described for opening dialogic space or diffusing conflict, for example, can be applied elsewhere, such as in families or friendship circles.

Second, groups vary in their **relative permanence**. I belong in my family and culture through my whole life. In fact, that group lasts far longer than my lifetime. Other groups might also last longer than my lifetime but my membership might not be permanent while I am alive. I might be a member of a choir for only a year, though the choir lasts for many more years. I belong in my work team for as long as I stay in that job and the organisation continues to structure itself in that way. Some groups are set up for specific purposes for very limited times. I might join a therapy group to combat depression, which runs for two hours a week over 6 or 12 weeks. I might join a workshop or focus group which is only one meeting of two or three hours. There are developmental perspectives (see Chapter 4) for all of these time dimensions. It is important for a facilitator to consider the developmental shape of a group and this will be very different depending on its lifespan.

Third, there is the issue of **size**. There is little correspondence between a nation and a five-person workgroup. The nuclear family tends to be relatively small, the extended family much larger. In naturally occurring groups size is not necessarily a variable which can be deliberately controlled; in constructed groups size is a matter for conscious control. Organisations tend to grow bigger over time because of theories about economies of scale, although bigger size is not necessarily more efficient (Locality/Vanguard 2014). Certainly, any large organisation will need to be broken down into smaller sub-units; hence the ubiquity of teams and departments.

All else being equal, our individual efficacy and sense of personal safety is much greater in a small group than in a large one. In a constructed group, meeting as a whole, if input is wanted from every individual, a group size of two to five is needed; as soon as it gets larger some individuals might remain silent. This usually means that to increase interactive participation some times of smaller 'group work' are needed. I, personally, like to start with a period of individual reflection to allow people to commune with themselves, before moving to small and then larger group involvement. In a team it is useful if people have opportunity to work with each other in subsets of two or three and for these groupings to vary regularly. This creates greater overall team cohesion.

How does one make opportunities for group work in very large, even global, organisations? Too discrete and boundaried a division into sub-units results in competing viewpoints and undermines the achievement of organisational unity and efficacy. There has been a rise, since the 1970s, of very large group interventions (Bunker & Alban 1997), which are designed to engage all levels of the organisation and also external stakeholders. This has had a further impetus in more recent times as a result of internet technologies. Some groups in this movement can be in excess of 1000 people and can even spread across the globe. However, the principles of size management by subdivision into smaller working groups still apply.

The **internet group** is in some ways a new phenomenon but in fact follows the same principles as a face-to-face group and requires the same facilitator skills. Some teams now might be geographically dispersed. Their only way of practising team-ness might be through internet contact. The facilitator still needs to attend to the participation of every member and should be vigilant to ensure that all have a voice and feel confident to express their viewpoints, even if at odds with the others. Of course there are no visual facilitation cues, unless using a video conferencing technology, and even in this case visual cues are minimised. There might also be a greater diversity of culture and even some language complications, which must be taken into account. Those less fluent in the language of common use must be given particular consideration and attention, to ensure that their real meaning is as understood as possible. The group size should remain small or be split into sub-groups who interact together and who are mixed from time to time to interact in other configurations.

Larger, non-team internet groups are often less facilitated than this. There are many special interest chat groups in which the majority of members probably do remain silent most of the time. Even these groups need a moderator, whose duty it is to ensure that the material being posted is non-offensive and relevant. Blogging supplies another internet way of communicating which looks individual rather than group on the face of it, but in fact many have possibilities of input from readers and a group often gathers around a particular blog.

In very large internet groups which are multiple and overlapping, such as social networking sites, there is minimal facilitation and members have to take their own responsibility to maintain boundaries. It is interesting to speculate that some problems of internet social networking might be because of a confusion between small group safety and the de facto presence of a huge group. Maybe when tweeting or when posting photographs, for example, some forget that the relational space is not small, safe and intimate (me, in my bedroom, with my laptop) but rather potentially vast.

Some groups are **open** and some are **closed**. In an open group membership varies over the life of the group; people come and go. In a closed group, which usually has a defined and limited lifespan, the same members are there for the whole life of the group. There might be attrition as some drop out but no new members will be admitted. Facilitation tasks are often easier for closed groups, as a developmental line is clearer. In open groups provision must be made for the adding of new members who do not share the history and (group) culture of members who have been there for a while.

FOR REFLECTION

- For the groups you considered earlier, reflect on these dimensions. Were they open or closed, permanent or temporary, how large?
- Did you include internet groups? How does facilitation work in the internet groups you belong to? Is it effective and how could it be more so?

The dimension of function

Let us now consider the function of the group as a dimension. No grouping is without function, whether explicit or implicit. What need is the group primarily designed to meet? This question might be comparatively difficult to answer in the case of large natural groups, though even for a nation, for example, the question could be answered – defence, economic mutuality and so on. The family, like the nation, is an example of a natural group with many functions, including emotional support, education, acculturation, economic and practical support. These are natural groups. In constructed groups there is usually a primary stated function, though there are probably other functions as well. As I argue, there should at least be a life-enhancing effect for members, as well as the stated purpose.

Is the group designed primarily to meet an external (e.g. organisational) need or the needs of the group members? There is a circularity in this external/internal dimension of function, as I have indicated above. Where there is a stated function of the welfare and development of members (e.g. therapy, development or supervision groups), this can only happen if the group as a whole provides a suitable milieu and the facilitator/leader attends to the welfare and development as tasks. Where the stated function is to achieve some task or specific, possibly organisational, purpose (e.g. focus groups, work teams, committees), if members are not empowered and allowed to release their own creativity and contribution to the group effort, they will give no added value.

Brown (2000) refers to much research on the perennial issue of whether a group really gives an advantage to a task or whether an individual or aggregate of individuals will achieve better. There are many variables which impact on this, not the least being whether members are from an individualistic culture where competition is highly valued or a collectivist culture where collaboration is more important. Group work tends to be more successful in the latter. I believe that the group micro-culture can be deliberately moved towards this collaborative spirit, even in a generally individualistic macro-culture. I believe that the creation of a supportive and collaborative culture is also best for the individual personal growth of group members.

The dimension of theory base

What is the theory base for the group? Management theories tend to be very task-centred, specifically concerned with efficiency and achievement outcomes. In other areas of endeavour the outcomes for the individual take precedence. In learning, training and supervision groups, the advancement of individual competence and knowledge is the primary task, sometimes in the service of a wider task demand (such as in apprenticeship training). In therapeutic groups members need to achieve psychological benefits, either in specific areas (e.g. assertiveness, dealing with depression) or in their perceived overall social and psychological functioning.

What are the effects of these models on group process? As indicated above, task-centred theories might miss the importance of intra-group dynamics. In therapy, individual theories of pathology might create negative and even hostile processes. Alternatively therapeutic theory might also ignore the group completely and focus on what the individual achieves and how to convey that material, thus being a sub-set of task-centred theory and missing the power of the relational space for enhancement or hindrance.

Groups are always an opportunity for growth of self-esteem and self-efficacy but can also be the opposite, destructive. We expand in confidence when people listen carefully to us and seem to value our contributions. We think and learn more efficiently when we are sufficiently relaxed and our universal tendency to social anxiety is minimised, though high emotional intensity can imprint material more deeply. If that emotional intensity is in a situation where we are defensive and disempowered we will be more inclined to hostility and negative stories about ourselves and others. If it is accompanied by sup-port and respect it makes us more confident in our own identity and more able to connect with others. Relative power has a part in this as well. The group leader/facilitator has a high-status position which can be used for good or harm.

The dimension of leadership style

There is a considerable body of knowledge in the literature about what qualities and attachment styles are optimal and what can be actually harmful in a group leader. The qualities of a good group leader have been more extensively studied in the organisational con-text but, interestingly, there is convergent information from the field of therapeutics.

An early study by Lippett and White in 1943 (Brown 2000) com-pared three styles of leadership: democratic, autocratic and laissez-faire. Unsurprisingly, the democratic leaders were best liked, followed by the laissez-faire ones. The autocratic leaders were least liked and tended to imbue groups with greater aggression, leader dependence and self-centredness but their groups worked hardest **while the leaders were present**. Work tended to stop when they were absent. Democratic lead-ers had friendly and reasonably task-oriented groups who would also work when the leader was absent. In groups with laissez-faire leaders there was least work accomplished, often with demands for more clar-ity. These groups worked **better** when the leader was absent. Clearly, from these findings, a democratic style of leadership was generally to be preferred.

In 1950 Bales propounded a concept of the task specialist versus the socio-emotional specialist, seeing these roles as usually being taken by different individuals. However, in the Ohio leadership studies the relationship between the two roles was seen as orthogonal. 'The best leader, it seemed, was the person who was rated above average on both attributes: someone who could organize the group's activities while remaining responsive to their views and feelings' (Brown 2000, p. 95). This model of the best leader ties up with the previous concept of a democratic leader. The Ohio studies found that of these attributes the most essential was the leader's ability to show a high level of consideration. 'A high level of consideration by the leader may help to offset too little concern with structure, but the reverse may not be true. However concerned with structure one is, one cannot compensate for a complete absence of consideration.' The effect was robust across cultures, though expressed differently in different cultures (Brown 2000, p. 96).

Yalom and Leszcz (2005, pp. 536–537) refer to a 1973 study on encounter groups where factor analysis of leadership behaviour variables yielded four functions: (1) emotional activation, (2) caring, (3) meaning attribution and (4) executive function. Of these, (2) and (3) had a linear relationship to positive outcome. Functions (1) and (4) had a curvilinear relationship to outcome; too little or too much were less useful. The authors conclude, 'The most successful leaders then – and this has great relevance for therapy – were those whose style was moderate in amount of stimulation and in expression of executive function and high in caring and meaning attribution.'

Attachment style is a theoretical construct which has generated a considerable body of research. We discuss this theory and its relationship to group dynamics in Chapter 2. It suffices here to say that the attachment style of the group leader has been shown to be important to the functioning of the group as a whole (e.g. Davidovitz et al. 2007). These authors found that, 'Leaders' attachment anxiety was associated with more self-serving leadership motives and with poorer leadership qualities in task-oriented situations. Leaders' attachment anxiety also predicted followers' poorer instrumental functioning. Leaders' attachment-related avoidance was negatively associated with prosocial motives to lead, with the failure to act as a security provider, and with followers' poorer socioemotional functioning and poorer long-range mental health.'

It is interesting how convergent the results are from these very different areas of research into group leadership. In summary, it is essential for group leaders/facilitators to be caring and not defensive of their own positions. If they are securely attached and confident of their own supports they are more able to support the functioning and emotional health of group members. Clarity of task structuring is also important, though not as important as their care for the people involved.

So, what can leaders do if they do not fit the ideal? I believe that before entering into a leadership or facilitation role we should evaluate our own attachment style.

Do I notice that I am over-sensitive to how people react to me? Do I have a strong need for affirmation but feel that I do not always get it? Do the people around me seem to slip between very close and supportive and very rejecting and cold? Do I sometimes embarrass myself by revealing too much of my vulnerability to those who then seem not to support me enough? Do I seem to take up too much talking time, focused on me and my issues? I might well have an anxious attachment style.

On the other hand, do I seem to encounter unexplained hostilities? Do I dislike emotional interaction with others? Is it difficult for me to understand where someone else is coming from; it seems so obvious that my position is correct that I distrust their motives and honesty if they disagree? Does it seem important for me not really to trust but to hide my feelings and any vulnerabilities? Or do I not have any vulnerabilities; if there's a problem it's because of what someone else is doing? Chances are I have an avoidant attachment style.

If I review my early experiences and the rules I set for myself as a small child I can further explore my own attachment style. If I really want a more 'objective' measure I can use a self-report adult attachment measure – they are available on the internet.

If I find that I do not have a secure attachment style there are things I can do about that, both in terms of altering it and in terms of managing my relationships in the light of how I relate. Entering into personal therapy focused on this issue is one possibility. In any event, when interacting I can bear in mind what my natural bias is and how that might be a filter for reality which I need to guard against.

For both anxiously attached and avoidant leaders, a very structured and task-focused group is easier. As we discussed above, strong task focus makes interactions less intrusive, as long as it is married with a rule of consideration for others. The idea of the 'servant leader' should be held as a primary guide to leadership interactions.

So, it is important for group leaders/facilitators to evaluate their own style. This should be done before engaging in a leadership or facilitator role but should also be ongoing. Using the Attachment model is one way of doing this, though other models can also be used. Do I say too much or too little? Am I too directive, leaving too little space for the ideas of others? Or am I not directive enough, making others feel confused and uncontained? Am I afraid to confront or am I too confrontational?

Any leaders or facilitators should constantly review and critique themselves in this way. Having their own personal supervision or mentoring is one way of checking, and it is useful if the supervisor or mentor can observe the process of actual live or recorded interaction to aid this review. It is also useful to get ongoing review from group participants. In management this is sometimes supplied through the 360° method of evaluation. This is a method where feedback is sought from leaders' managers but also from those they lead. For therapists this can be obtained from clients; at least at the end of the treatment, as a final evaluation.

FOR REFLECTION

- Evaluate your own attachment style, using the above information (and other means, if required).
- What will be the impact of your own style on how you might facilitate a group? What structures might you need to put in place?
- What will you need to attend to in order to maximise your facilitative effectiveness?
- Who could support your development in this area, and how?

Evaluating the group

Evaluation is an important part of group process. What evaluations should happen and when?

The evaluation of the task is often built into the process, at least in business. A business plan includes objective and measurable markers on a timeline so that progress can be clearly measured. Sometimes this use of a business plan cannot be filtered down in as clear terms at the level of teams and departments. Some of them can show concrete measures but sometimes the nature of the task is such that they cannot. In therapy groups the progress is often judged by the use of measuring instruments, such as questionnaires, which try to capture reduction in symptoms, and so on. It is probably obvious to all that some sort of measurement of task is essential.

What about that other function of groups, their interactive and social health? This is less frequently measured and relies on the subjective perceptions of the members. This class of measurement could be dismissed as irrelevant by business leaders and even by therapists who believe that the interaction should just be allowed to develop spontaneously, and especially if they believe that conflict and interpersonal tensions are inevitable and self-resolving.

I believe that every group which has a life of more than a few hours should build in periodic, frequent reviews of the extent of group cohesiveness and how members are feeling, especially in regard to their enthusiasm for the group and its purposes and their sense of whether they are able to make a significant and appreciated contribution to task. Some teams plan away days and special meetings where this can be evaluated. However such meetings can easily slide into avoiding the interpersonal dynamics by focusing on presentations and news-giving at the expense of interaction and an exploration of personal responses. If it really seems too difficult to deal with these, it is important to use the services of a competent external facilitator.

Certainly, it is a task of the leader, manager, group therapist or facilitator to assess dynamics on an ongoing basis by exploring either with the group as a whole or with the individuals who make up the group. It is also important that reviews are fed back to the group so that all can take responsibility for making improvements and celebrating what is going well.

FOR REFLECTION

- Think of one of the groups you belong to. What gets reviewed or evaluated?
- Do you believe any other kind of review or evaluation should happen?
- How would you design this review or evaluation?

Summary: why this book, and how is it structured?

We have seen that human beings spend most of their waking lives in groups; all of their waking lives if we include their families and cultures in our analysis. These are kinds of naturally occurring groups. We also spend much time in specially constructed groups, usually set up for specific purposes or functions. These groups might last for only one or two hours, for a few weeks, a few months, years or even beyond our lifespan.

Group members, but even more so group leaders, can facilitate process so that both task achievement and interpersonal dynamics are optimised. This can only happen if they attend both to task, with its structuring, and to what is happening emotionally between and within the group members. They also need to be modelling care, consideration and non-defensiveness. It is important to set up a positive group culture, not to assume, 'That's not my business,' or that nothing can be done about conflict, dissatisfaction and patterns which are destructive either to function or participants. This book collects what is known about creating a 'best possible' group culture and describes principles and techniques for achieving this which my colleagues and I have used in many different contexts.

Chapters 2 and 3 describe the theory base for a Systemic-Narrative approach to group dynamics; Systemic ideas are laid out in Chapter 2 and Narrative ones in Chapter 3. Chapters 4 and 5 are the 'how to' chapters, with models for starting a group, setting and keeping the culture and what to do about specific process problems. Chapter 6 contains recorded conversations illustrating some uses of the approach.

2

BASICS OF SYSTEMIC THINKING AND GROUPS AS AN ECOLOGY OF MINDS

Thinking systemically

Joe has just started school and is difficult to manage there. He doesn't interact well with the other children and constantly demands the attention of the teacher. His family say he is perfectly well behaved at home and feel there is something wrong at school. The school feel that there is something very wrong with the family.

They are referred to a family therapist who notes that Joe is an only child and the household includes five adults: Joe's parents, one set of grandparents and an uncle. She hypothesises that the problem here is neither in the school system nor in the family system but in the interface between the two systems. The school agree to allocate a bit more adult attention to him until he settles. The family begin to make a practice of inviting other children or encouraging him to visit other children where there is less adult attention. The problem is soon solved and he settles well.

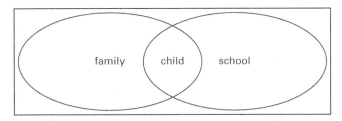

Figure 2.1 Interaction between Joe's systems

Here is an example of systemic thinking. If Joe were considered simply as an individual child, without taking into account his environment (two contrasting environments in this case) he could soon attract

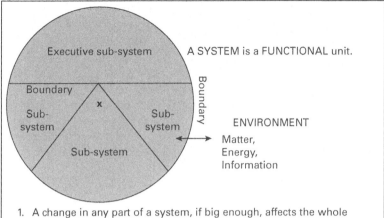

1. A change in any part of a system, if big enough, affects the whole system.
2. All else being equal, a change in the executive sub-system has the most impact.
3. Small changes in different parts of a system can be additive.

Figure 2.2 Basic systemic concepts

un-useful labels, like 'attention-seeking' or even 'ADHD'. Note also that the existence of the problem makes people in both groups or social systems (the school and the family) begin to create negative narratives about the other group. This seeds a problem in between-group dynamics which may easily become permanent, with parents becoming increasingly dissatisfied with the school and educators becoming increasingly convinced that the child has emotional difficulties because of having a dysfunctional family.

More about between-group dynamics later in this chapter. First let's define some terms as they are used throughout this book.

A **system** is a functional unit made up of interacting elements. For example, the cardiovascular system is made up of heart, blood vessels and blood and has the **function** of transport for its **environment**, the body. Each of the interacting elements in a system can be thought of as **subsystems**. So, in this example, the heart is one sub-system (with its own functions) of the cardiovascular system, the arteries are another, and so on.

Similarly, social groups can be seen as systems. For example, a school could be seen as a system within the environment of education provision, with subsystems of administration, teachers and students. A nuclear family is a system with two subsystems in respect of most functions; parents and children.

All systems exchange matter, energy or information with their environments and these exchanges also happen between subsystems across a **boundary**. The boundary simply defines what is or is not part of the system but boundaries may be more or less permeable. Some systems are relatively closed to the environment, some more open. Again, the concept can be applied to subsystems as well.

The **executive subsystem** is the management subsystem in respect of any function; the subsystem with the most executive power to drive forward or change that function. Generally, this applies to most functions of the system. In a nuclear family this would be the parental subsystem. In an organisation it would be the top management. However, there might be an executive subsystem which is different from the usual one in respect of a particular function. If the issue (function) were one of worker activism, for example, trade union officials might comprise the executive subsystem in an organisation. It is useful to think in terms of power differential when looking at any social system.

FOR REFLECTION

- Think of your family, your work team and any other group to which you belong.
- What subsystems (in terms of their FUNCTION) can you identify?
- What are some ways in which these groups, seen as systems, interact with the environment? Are they relatively open or closed to the environment (boundary more or less permeable)?
- Who constitutes the executive subsystem in each? How well do the executive subsystems function and why?

A frequent problem brought to systemic thinkers is dysfunction, or lack of unified team working, within the executive subsystem. Management might be split. A parent might be in coalition with a child in opposition to the other parent. Good facilitation is required to free the executive subsystem for its required purposes.

A voluntary organisation was dangerously hampered by a board of trustees split over the direction which the organisation should be taking. The chairman had strong beliefs about developing in one direction which the treasurer and two other influential board members thought ill-advised. As a consequence there was a stagnation of activity and the threat of loss of funding. Consultants were engaged to facilitate a board away day for the development of a business plan. Opposing views were aired in a more reflective space and a compromise solution was achieved, leading to a clear plan of action and renewed vigour.

The system diagram also shows three rules of change. They are very freeing. Previously, in psychotherapeutic work, if individual *x* had a problem which could not be resolved by direct work with him (either with his biological systems, by medication, etc. or in his inter-psychic or cognitive systems), the situation was stuck.

Systemic thinking meant that the social context of that individual could also become a focus of intervention; particularly, but not exclusively, the emotionally important system of the family. Interventions in this system generated change for the individual. They could be made anywhere within the system and could constitute either one large change or several small ones. These would then generate enough change for the individual to move forward. For example, early work on high Expressed Emotion (EE) (Vaughn & Leff 1985) has proved very robust in dealing with psychosis. These authors found that people suffering from psychosis were much more likely to relapse if there was a lot of intensity and negativity in the family; if they were treated with criticism rather than compassion. We have known since that modifying how a family manages the illness can give a better prognosis.

Another advantage of systemic thinking was the opportunity offered for collaboration with those in the system, thus widening the available knowledge base for effective and positive change.

Martha had a serious Obsessive Compulsive Disorder (OCD) and Agoraphobia. She refused to go to see any services about this but was extremely controlling, even violent, towards her elderly, frail parents. They were often prevented from going out of the house themselves because she became hysterically anxious and hung onto them. They spent many hours helping her to complete her checking rituals.

Eventually they themselves consulted a therapist who was prepared to work with them without being able to meet the Identified Patient (IP). They became more understanding and less angry with their daughter. Simultaneously, by small steps they started becoming firmer in recovering their own lives and refusing to collaborate in the OCD culture, gently explaining to her the principle which underlies all treatment of Anxiety, to push gently and gradually against it.

Their lives and her independence improved. She eventually agreed to go herself to see the therapist. Finally she was able to go out, get work and block for herself the checking behaviours.

We see from the above example that intervention in a group or system can be made wherever it is possible to intervene. It is possible to work with whoever is motivated to do so or feels able to do so. Unfortunately, many helping organisations are still focused on the **Identified Patient (IP)** and are not geared up to work with the natural group of people to which that IP belongs. In any family, group or team it may not be possible to collaborate with a particular individual. In systemic thinking this does not matter; the necessary change can happen in a different part of the system.

FOR REFLECTION

- Think of a group with one very difficult member who doesn't respond directly to intervention from the facilitator.
- How might the facilitator work with the group as a whole or with another member to improve the input from that difficult member?

Another truism of systemic thinking is the principle· **when stuck, widen the system.** If a nuclear family gets stuck, widening to include the extended family or a support agency might be useful. Social services, for example, might become involved. More creatively, other parts of the community could be considered; church, voluntary organisations, friends. Several therapeutic treatment approaches, especially when risk is high, include others from outside the system of interest (e.g. Cooper & Vetere 2005, Omer 2004). In an organisational context the same might happen if consultants are brought in, restructuring occurs, or if a team boundary is made more permeable.

Here follows an example of widening the system in a work group context:

Pat was totally frustrated by the small team she worked in. Her department was made up of herself and two colleagues, one of whom was the lead and had many more years of experience in their field. Both colleagues seemed to her more interested in sitting in the office discussing fashion than in getting out and doing the work. She felt judged for her own more active approach and had no one to discuss her ideas with.

She heard about a county-wide group of people involved in the same field, and in desperation, joined it. In this group she found many colleagues who shared her passions and way of tackling the work. This made her regain her confidence. It also made her able to draw in visiting professionals, who in turn eventually influenced her lead. Their working styles and concerns became less disparate.

FOR REFLECTION

- Think of a recent problem which occurred in a group (team, family, etc.) you belong to.
- Could widening the system have helped? How might you have done this?

Relationships, process and circular causality

We tend to think of causality in linear terms: A causes B. This simple view of cause and effect is generally valid. I press the A key and A appears on the screen. I drop a glass which hits the floor and breaks. Pressing the key gave a particular result on the screen. Dropping the glass caused it to break. Even this type of description is, of course, too simple. There is a causality chain between pressing the A and the icon on screen; with a different keyboard setup or a faulty computer I might get a different icon. The glass might fall on something soft and not break. Nevertheless, the direction of causality is clear.

Partly, this is because a subject (the operator) is interacting with an object. If two or more subjects interact the situation becomes much more complex because they are both (all) acting and reacting to the other/s simultaneously. This creates what systemic theorists call **circular causality**. Every action is simultaneously a cause and a result of the other's action.

Children can often be found arguing, 'You started it'. Unfortunately adults can still be trapped into this kind of thinking. With reflection we realise that even before any specific action takes place there are precursors to both action and reaction in our biology, culture, experiences.

FOR REFLECTION

- Think of a time you felt in conflict with someone and wanted them to change.
- Letting go of any idea of changing the other person, how could you have changed what you were doing or thinking?
- How might this have changed the way the situation felt for you?
- Would there have been a change of outcome?

Even when we meet a stranger, the situation is not neutral. We immediately start to model ideas about that person based on our previous experiences, and of course that person is doing the same about us. Much of this modelling or theorising happens at a relatively unconscious level. As a nursery rhyme tells us,

> I do not like thee, Dr Fell,
> The reason why I cannot tell
> But this I know, and know full well,
> I do not like thee, Dr Fell.

Or we might automatically like him. If we think long and hard we will realise that this is because he reminds us of someone else we knew before, who was experienced either as pleasant or unpleasant. Or maybe he belongs to a group of which our family had strong and possibly fixed opinions. As we get to know Dr Fell better we continue to modify our ideas about him. Sadly, it is possible that our first ideas (and his about us) caused us to respond to each other in a way which develops into a dysfunctional interaction.

Systemic neutrality is often seen as essential for a therapist or facilitator. As we can tell from this discussion, we are never really neutral. We automatically like some people more than others and we easily find ourselves taking a particular side in a discussion or argument. It is vital for facilitators, however, to be reflective and flexible about this, to hold our opinions, alliances and prejudices loosely. We have to be prepared to like Dr Fell. We have to query our most built-in assumptions. Minuchin (1974) argued that the systemic therapist needs to become aligned with different members of the group at different times and be ready to move in and out of intense involvement with the whole family (group).

Freud developed some ideas about the interaction between a therapist and client. The client was said to project onto the therapist a model of interaction which mirrored his relationship with his parents and this was termed the **transference**. Later psychoanalytical thinkers widened the term so that it included patterns of interaction developed with others as well as the parents. The response of the therapist to this transference, presumably also mediated by former experiences, was named the **counter-transference.**

It was useful to note the impact of former or habitual ways of responding to someone else but the concept of transference and counter-transference constrains our thinking in some very important ways. First, it applies only to the relationship within a **dyad** (two-person group), in this instance between client and therapist. Incidentally it feeds into the concept of the non-interacting or *tabula rasa* therapist, whose position is to make a blank screen onto which the client can best project those earlier relationships.

However, this tabula rasa stance is relationally strange. One of the dyad (the client, in this style of therapy) might very well be extremely threatened by the other's not responding in an expected human way. The type of response being projected could look much more dysfunctional than the client's usual response. In *Group 1* (Chapter 1) the facilitator is taking a tabula rasa position and the group members are reacting defensively.

More constraining, however, is the linear nature of the concept. It implies a therapist who is always only in the reactive position to attitudes initiated by the client. Linear, not circular, causality.

For a systemic thinker a more useful model is that of **process**. The process is the pattern of interacting and can apply between therapist and client or client and client or indeed among group members. That pattern may either be in the immediate interaction (**within-session process**) or that which takes place over longer periods of time. Process is never static; it can be seen as a dance in which each participant brings habits and previous experiences, interacting with the other/s uniquely. As the dance (process) continues it is modified and new experiences give rise to new habits.

FOR REFLECTION

- Think about how you interact with another particular person.
- Do you see yourself as reacting to their behaviour or do they react to yours?
- How does this interaction change in the presence of another person you know?
- Has your relationship changed over time? How?

In the systemic tradition **triads** have been of greater interest than dyads. Groups could be modelled as sets of interlocking triads. A interacts differently with B in the presence of C. Actually, even this is limiting but there is a difficulty with how much complexity we can model. In a group, A's interaction with B might be differently modified by the presence of C if D is also present! We could get lost in an intricate cat's cradle but the principle is clear; relationships are always influenced by other relationships.

Triadic concepts were famously propounded early in the development of family therapy by Minuchin (1974) when he proposed some patterns of a child's involvement with its parent's conflicts. An early process observation in family therapy was that, as the emotional intensity escalates, a child (often even a very young child or infant) will begin some disruptive behaviour, thus cutting through or deflecting potential conflict. This behaviour is produced automatically (therefore subconsciously) because what is happening is more threatening than being seen as naughty. The gains in felt safety and family peace may come at a cost to that child, whose behaviour might be labelled as symptomatic in some way, without consideration of its context. Alternatively, some children may develop a more gentle peacemaker role.

The pattern doesn't only relate to making peace when parents are in conflict, of course. Even in the above scenario, another child might be seen always to leave the scene when conflict starts to happen, having developed an internal rule that it is better to avoid conflictual situations. Children develop customary ways of dealing with parents, siblings, peers, in various situations. Some might become quiet and 'invisible'. Some learn to be the 'life and soul of the party'. Some learn that aggression is often useful, or whining, or 'people pleasing'. Typically they carry on these patterns of managing interactions for the rest of their lives.

FOR REFLECTION

- What are your habitual ways of reacting in groups?
- Can you identify early experiences in which you might have found these habits functional?
- Is there any way or situation in which you might want to modify these habits now?

We all develop strategies for managing through life and these process patterns make up a large part of our 'personality', or habitual ways of relating. Because these process patterns are often developed very early in life and are applied automatically, or unconsciously, they may also be applied in situations where they are not functional. They will almost certainly play out when we are in groups of people. Different groups, however, might bring out different process patterns in the same person. There are also some universals about how we all react. For example, any perceived attack will be met with defensiveness; we just might have different ways of doing that defence. Some people, like Jill in **Group 1** (Chapter 1), become quiet, unwilling to reveal anything about themselves. Others, like Maggie, become loud and argumentative.

It is important to remember that although these patterns are played out largely unconsciously they can become the focus of conscious attention and modified. Our habits have force and can be a default position but habits can be changed by conscious attention and practice.

FOR REFLECTION

- Think of a time recently when you became defensive in a group of people. How did you react?
- How could you have done things differently?
- What would have made the situation feel safe enough for you not to react defensively?

Multiple generations: process patterns through time

Family practitioners became interested early in ideas about the developmental stages of a family and also in what patterns in families prevailed across generations. Some of our most observable ways of interacting with others reflect what has happened historically in our families. Using **genograms**, a kind of family tree (see below), they started mapping how relationships had worked over the generations. John Byng-Hall (1988) became interested in the stories families have about themselves over more than one generation. He particularly conceived the idea of **replicative** and **corrective scripts.** These are particular kinds of the largely unconscious process patterns we have discussed in this chapter. In a replicative script we do things in the same way as our parents or family because that just seems, in our family culture, to be 'the way you do it'. In a corrective script you disagree with the way the family did things and tend to do the opposite.

Group work and the group as an ecology of minds

Much of what is described as **group dynamics** in relational space is made up of the interplay of these habitual patterns by individuals. **Group roles** often reflect roles that we habitually take elsewhere.

> *In a mixed Eating Disorders therapeutic group of seven women, certain roles begin to emerge. Ann is a very caring, motherly woman. She soon takes Lisa under her wing. Lisa has a background of having been horrifically abused and is very vulnerable. She attaches to Ann as the fantasy perfect mother she always wanted. Meanwhile, Mary is talkative and extrovert, seeming always to be cheerful and often deflects attention to herself when anyone seems sad or angry. Phyllis is quiet and reveals little of herself but seems depressed and cynical about the potential value of the group. Joan and Sarah knew each other prior to the group and sit together, inclined to gossip about village affairs rather than being fully involved in the focus of the group work. Kate is the 'hard worker', always earnestly doing what is required and seeming to want a collegiate relationship with the facilitator.*
>
> ***Group 2***

This description is of a therapeutic group but whatever the group purpose, it is the job of the facilitator/leader/manager to notice the roles being adopted by different individuals and consider how these can best meet the needs both of the group task and of each group member. Roles might be utilised or modified. Above all, it is important to remember that they are not in themselves dysfunctional. On the contrary, they are habits of relating which members have chosen for their perceived utility. They also do not completely define the individuals who enact them. The facilitator's mind is interpreting and analysing what is taking place in the room but so is every other mind present. Members will only modify their own roles or ideas based on their own interpretations and motivation.

FOR REFLECTION

- Analyse a group you know in terms of the customary roles taken by participants.
- Do you know if some of these people have different roles in other groups?
- How are roles useful in the group?
- How might they need to be modified and how could this happen?

The founder of modern hypnotism, who also had a profound influence in the field of family therapy, Milton Erickson, taught **utilisation** (Haley 1973), the idea that rather than trying to stop what is happening you use what is there, changing gently as needed. Haley points out that if you try to stop a flow of water it will engulf you, whereas you can divert its course. In the following example the tutor employs utilisation. Joe's role is diverted, while his personality and abilities remain the same, like those of Paul after his conversion on the road to Damascus.

A high school class was very difficult to manage. The tutor noted that Joe was usually the ringleader. He had a problem with dyslexia and this fomenting of trouble was clearly a way for him to gain status among his peers and mend his self-respect. Efforts to discipline Joe had singularly failed. It seemed that the more detentions and exclusions he accumulated the worse his behaviour became.

The tutor found an opportunity to meet informally with Joe and congratulated him on his leadership ability. He pointed out that the rest of the class were likely to follow as Joe led and requested his help in driving through a particular project. They then met at other times to review the progress of the project. Later, further projects were added in. Joe learned to put his leadership abilities to pro-social rather than anti-social uses and ultimately gained respect in a healthier way. Class dynamics and general behaviour improved vastly!

Attachment styles and group process

One way of modelling the responses of individuals to the group is to examine their **attachment styles**. Ideas about attachment were first propounded by Bowlby, who noted that infants would explore their environment with curiosity and enjoyment in the presence of an adult with whom they felt secure. If that adult left the room, however, their anxiety would rise and they would replace exploratory behaviour with safety seeking. Further investigation suggested that the ongoing relationship of an infant with primary carers (usually but not necessarily parents, especially mother) gives rise to habitual ways of relating to the world. Infants who find that the carer is reliably available develop a relaxed and trusting approach to the world. They are able to be generally secure, with their attention focused on curiosity and creativity. This pattern became labelled **secure attachment**. When the care was arbitrary, sometimes available and sometimes withheld, the child became anxious and intensely care-seeking, often clingy and whiny. This was labelled **anxious attachment.** If the carer was generally distant and cold, unresponsive to messages of need, the child seemed to deny the need for any attachment, becoming inexpressive and self-contained. This was labelled an **avoidant attachment** style.

Later research and theorising followed these attachment styles into adulthood. As we discussed above, processes of relating are often developed early in life and carried through as habits into adulthood. **Attachment** is a simple and useful way to model particular process patterns and their probable aetiology and has been the focus of a substantial body of research. Three adult attachment styles are therefore usually identified; **secure, anxious** and **avoidant.**

FOR REFLECTION

- Identify your own attachment style.
- How and why do you think it developed?
- What would help to move it towards a more secure style?

Within groups, the anxious and avoidant attachment styles have particular relevance. For both, perceived threats in the social environment create physiological arousal. People with the avoidant style become very detached from their own emotional processes as well as from those of others. They are literally unaware of their own emotions, whether positive or negative. By contrast, those with anxious styles are hyper-aware and ultra-sensitive to perceived threat or insult. Their emotions can swing very quickly. Both groups are using energy to regulate their emotional arousal and this means there is less energy available for the task, whether that task is an organisational aim or activity or whether it is the support of peers. Attempts at emotional regulation can also disturb good group process. It is not useful if people are unaware of their own or others' reactions. It is not useful if people demand extra consideration and support and have fluctuating, often incomprehensible emotional reactions. In Chapter 5 we consider more about how to deal with the fallout from these patterns.

What has therefore been of great interest to clinicians and researchers in recent years has been how to modify anxious and avoidant attachment, making them more secure. In longer-term therapies the therapist can be seen as an attachment figure and it is conceptualised that this dyadic relationship can modify or heal the dysfunctional effects of the early attachment trauma. Systemic therapists have accepted the concept of therapy as a **secure base** but have been more inclined to try to support the development of a secure base in the client's natural relationship network. For some adults or older children this change happens without therapy when 'corrective' relationships with authority figures or peers modify the expectations built up in early childhood (e.g. Benard 1991).

*John was a happy, secure child until the age of three years, when he developed an infectious illness and was removed from his parents to a sanatorium for six months **(attachment trauma)**. When he returned he was quiet and non-responsive (avoidant attachment). He retained this personality style into adulthood but fortunately made a good marriage with a warm, caring woman who thought (and continued to think) that he was wonderful. A few years into this marriage gave him a secure attachment style.*

Benard and others particularly emphasise that relationships in naturally occurring groups can create a secure attachment base. Clearly the same secure base can be deliberately engendered by careful and thoughtful facilitation of constructed groups, as in the following example.

Gina looks forward to her fortnightly development group with eagerness and relief. A passionate and committed worker, she had a difficult childhood and has an anxious attachment style. She began the group very sensitive to the attention of the others, but more particularly of the facilitator. Would he offer her sufficient care or would she have to work hard to retain his positive attention? She tried very hard at first to please him and be a 'good', participative group member. This carried the risk that she would annoy the others by her 'attention-seeking' behaviour and also that she might reveal too much very personal material too early in the development of the group, therefore becoming too exposed and increasing her attachment anxiety.

As time went on she became more and more relaxed. The facilitator gently blocked her from taking too much talking time, not by putting her down or embarrassing her but by inviting resonances and reflections from others. This practice and other exercises gradually produced more intimacy and security between participants so that the group itself is beginning to have the ripple effect of making her attachment patterns more secure.

Gerry learned early in life that adults were not reliably available to support him and that his best strategy was to be self-sufficient and secretive about his feelings. He learned this so well that he rarely knows himself what he feels. Actually, he is a poor candidate for group work but his manager has indicated that this group is compulsory. Never mind, he can attend but not participate!

The introductory exercises make him most uncomfortable and he considers leaving despite management pressure. However, he 'gets away with' participating superficially. As time goes on he finds that he is not required to voice his feelings and that the group seems to respect his ideas and ability to structure. Eventually, he responds marginally to the modelling of openness around him, becoming more open and expressive himself. Very slowly he learns that no one is putting him down or undermining him and he can begin to trust the group. His avoidant attachment moves towards secure attachment.

These two participants have been able to make gains because the facilitator is securely attached and knowledgeable about attachment styles and their different social requirements. In this safe context some specific and gentle confrontation of their accustomed patterns might eventually be applied by the facilitator or group members with the result of deepening their gains.

If the facilitator had been anxiously attached, Gina might have enjoyed the group and benefitted from it but the above dangers would apply with the additional one of possibly too permeable boundaries. Their dance of interacting needs and anxieties could result in insufficient reining in of Gina's emotional spilling, which could complicate her relationship with others, evoking a group split between those who are drawn into wanting to protect and nurture her and those who are made uncomfortable by her emotional intensity and reject her as 'manipulative'.

An avoidant facilitator is likely to have increased her anxiety by his unavailability, reminding her of the insecurities of her childhood. In this context she is more likely to find the group aversive and possibly to be harmed by it, and if confrontation occurs it could easily wound her and increase her insecurity.

Gerry could well find an insecure facilitator productive of the group of his worst nightmare; 'wallowing in the touchy-feely'. He would almost certainly have discontinued, whatever the pressure to engage, or at best would stay, feeling increasingly hostile and disengaged. An avoiding facilitator would be the most comfortable for him but would support or generate a group process in which he would not learn to engage more trustingly with others.

These are probable consequences of different facilitator/leader attachment styles but remember that we are over-simplifying for purposes of illustration. Different processes might affect outcomes. To assume that any event, style or process leads inevitably to any other with human beings is to revert to **linear thinking**, as discussed earlier.

FOR REFLECTION

- Consider again your own attachment style.
- What are the implications for you as a group member?
- What are the implications for you as a group facilitator?
- How can you ensure your good facilitation or participation even if your attachment style is anxious or avoidant?
- Consider again what might make it more secure, in the light of the above section.

Using genograms, eco maps and other diagrams

Often a diagram can be more effective than talk in clarifying tasks and process; therefore in helping a group to achieve both task and relationship. Organisations use flow charts and structural diagrams. CBT and other practitioners use diagrams to map interactions and behavioural loops.

In systemic worlds (family therapy, social work, etc.) there are two kinds of drawn diagrams, which are extremely useful and can be employed in various ways with different groups; the genogram and eco map. Of the two, the genogram is more widely known and probably more frequently used and has various conventions to aid in reading it. The eco map is less prescribed and more flexible; it might be said to be another label for any diagram mapping interactions. Rather like a mind map, it can diagram anything of interest. It is often used to show interacting social systems, as in the simple Venn-like diagram of the family, child and school earlier in this chapter. More standard eco maps show the household (or group) in a central circle with relationships between the members diagrammed according to a convention, and influences on each leading out from the circle.

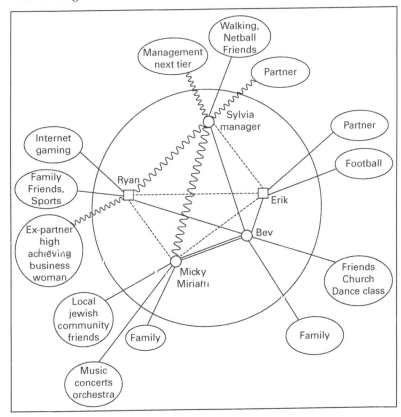

Genogram 2.1 Bev team eco map

Similarly, the genogram is often used. This is generally a 'family tree', again drawn within certain conventions, which are the same as those for eco maps. Generally, small squares represent males, small circles are females, a double line shows close connection and a zigzag line conflictual connection (McGoldrick et al. 1999). As with eco maps, many examples of genograms can be found on the internet. Whereas the eco map gives a snapshot of 'how things are at the moment', genograms add in the dimension of change and development over time. Most particularly, this time dimension is in a family (a family tree). Genograms have been drawn, however, showing the history of a field of ideas (McGoldrick et al. 1999) and could potentially map the history of a team or group.

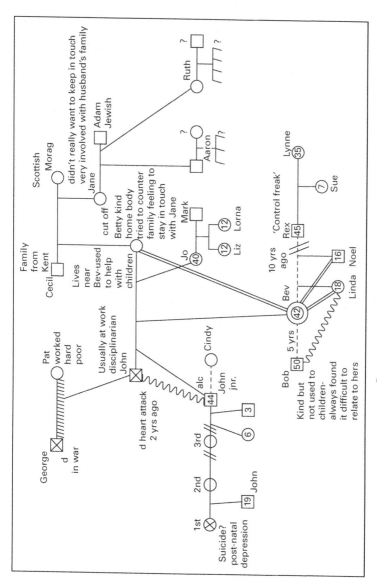

Genogram 2.2 Bev genogram

Genogram 2.1 is an example of an eco map. Bev is a member of a team whose manager is Sylvia. Sylvia is rather 'stressy', with tensions in her relationships with both the management above her and more particularly with her partner. Ryan has some responses which particularly madden Sylvia in her partner, so her relationship with him is also difficult. She also often seems to clash with Micky.

Eric gets along with everyone but doesn't make close or intense relationships. Ryan is most strongly involved in internet games but is friendly with all of his colleagues, except for his manager, Sylvia. Micky and Bev are more involved with and interested in their own families than anything else. In this team, Bev, who relates more positively to all the others than they tend to relate to each other, will probably find that she is the default facilitator and will need to take on that role to improve team functioning.

In our sample genogram, (2.2), imagining the same Bev, we see some possible reasons for her position in the team. Her strong closeness to Micky might well be a corrective script in response to the anti-Semitism in her maternal family, especially as her mother has already tried to apply that corrective script and she is very close to her mother. It is possible too that she is used to having to be a facilitator between her second husband and her children.

In groups, genograms can be used in various ways. In a fairly small group (say six or fewer individuals) all individuals can present their genograms to all other individuals as a way of deepening connections and illustrating similarities and differences in cultural background. In a larger group this can be done in pairs and the presentation can be more curtailed. Presenting our family feels less personal and intrusive than presenting our own life timeline, yet gives rich information about the ways of thinking which might seem obvious to us but far from obvious to others. John Byng-Hall (1988) pointed out that family scripts and legends are the 'Aesop's fables' for each generation. The themes which arise in our family stories show the tendencies and patterns which we will unconsciously apply to current life situations.

FOR REFLECTION

- Do your own genogram and consider some family scripts, for example, around gender roles.
- How do you play out these scripts in other groups?

McGoldrick and colleagues (1999) show that genograms might not be only of families. A team could draw its genogram, showing the history of its development and the individuals and their ideas involved. Organisational engagement methods often begin with a charting of history as a base for launching into the future (Bunker & Alban 1997) and a genogram-style mapping could be useful for this part of the process.

Sculpts and action methods

Just as diagrams and pictures might add an important dimension to purely verbal communication in groups, so might action methods. One such method, which was popularised in the systemic field, though it is less used than it perhaps should be, is the **sculpt**. In this technique, protagonists place themselves within the room in a physical relationship to each other which reflects their felt psychological space. For example, if someone is seen as more powerful, that person could be up on a chair or table. Those experiencing oppression could crouch in a defensive position. Those who feel distanced will stand further away than those who feel close. People might stand with their backs to the action, or looking straight into it, they might link arms or stand in a combative posture.

Sculpts can be of the current situation or show a **preferred future**. They could be directed by particular individuals; for example, to illustrate the differences between how two individuals perceive a situation – in this case each would create the sculpt in turn and a following discussion would look at how the felt circumstances were different or the same. Alternatively, all protagonists can place themselves in the position and attitude which reflects their own feelings. This is usually more manageable with big groups.

FOR REFLECTION

- How would you sculpt a particular group you belong to?
- How might another member sculpt it?
- If you can, try actually doing this.

A sculpt or similar action method has the effect of getting past the talk and giving a more visceral experience of what is happening or what is wanted in the future. It can be followed by an exploration in words of what the experience felt like for those participating, or it can be left to speak for itself. The emotional impact and potential for opening out new ways of thinking is often surprising to participants.

Other psychodrama ideas can be used at times. People can act out the effects of **externalised** issues or **preferred future** scenarios can be acted out (see Chapter 3).

The **empty chair** technique, first propounded in the field of Gestalt Therapy, is well known but also often forgotten and very powerful. In this technique an empty chair is imagined to contain another person who is in fact not in the room and those present express what they want to say to that person. This can be used to express what might otherwise be left unsaid. As we will be discussing throughout this book, the more open and candid group members can be about what they are thinking, the better the group dynamics and task achievement will be.

A special development of these psychodrama ideas which has been popular in systemic circles is **internalised other interviewing**. In this technique, group members are interviewed as though they were someone else, possibly each other or possibly someone outside the group. We all have models in our own minds of how we see the minds of those with whom we are in relationship. Internalised other interviewing makes us develop and 'thicken' this model, resulting in an increase in empathy and available ideas.

> Gerald was tasked to improve staff practices in a care home for people with profound learning difficulties. Most of the residents could not speak and would often become very frustrated, acting out behaviourally. The staff felt powerless to control this behaviour and would feel angry and victimised themselves, resulting in a tense and punitive culture.
>
> Each staff member was allocated a resident and asked to come to a meeting prepared to 'be that person'. They were then interviewed 'as the resident' and asked what they felt when certain events happened, what it meant when they engaged in certain behaviours. For example, 'Yesterday, when you threw your food at Colin, what were you trying to say? Why did you decide to do that just then?' 'What makes it easiest for you to calm down in the evening so that you can get a good night's rest?'
>
> The intervention had the desired effect. Staff found that they could empathise much better: that the 'we and they' feeling broke down. This technique was paired with support for and understanding of how the staff themselves felt in the difficulties of their situation. The culture of the home changed for the better.

FOR REFLECTION

- In a pair with someone, ask them to interview you while you take the role of your partner, or someone else with whom you have a significant relationship.
- When you are answering 'as that person', what insights do you gain into their motivation?
- Does this increase your empathy and understanding? If it does, how might this be useful?

Summary: groups as social systems and ecologies of minds

As we have seen, there are many ways to model how people interact in groups. In the Systemic tradition we make use of General Systems Theory, which helps us to think of the interfaces between different systems (groups) and also about the social structures within those systems. Above all, it brings us the freeing principle that we can work with any part of a group to make a difference and that difference will affect the rest of the group. It is not always necessary to target change in 'the person who holds the problem'. Related to this is the rule that small changes in different parts of the group can be additive.

The complications of group dynamics can be modelled in various ways, all depending on observing the patterns of relating or **process**. As far back as Freud, the patterns between a therapist and client were of interest (dyadic process). This can now be expanded to think of triadic and wider processes; of the patterns which we develop early in our lives in our primary families and their modification through later relationships. A special modelling which is often the focus of attention and research today is that of Attachment Theory.

There are other ways of modelling interactions. The study of group roles is one. In a constructed group, we can see different individuals taking on different roles and often these are habitual. The experiences of their lives have persuaded them into those ways of reacting and interacting. Roles may be highly functional but may sometimes be dysfunctional. Thinking about them as habits of interaction both explains their tenacity and reminds us that habits can be changed, albeit with difficulty, by conscious attention.

The group is an 'ecology of minds': all groups are made up of individuals. There are infinite variations in what each individual might bring to the group, and its success, whether in tasks or interactions, is related to how individuals feel about participating. They are all, differentially, acting and reacting simultaneously in the social environment. It is primarily the facilitator who is responsible for promoting the safety and challenging of each person, taking into account issues of personal boundaries and the defended self of all kinds of participant.

NARRATIVE THEORY AND SOME BASICS OF HUMAN COMMUNICATION FOR OPTIMAL GROUP DYNAMICS

Social constructionism

Well, we have to begin this chapter with a short excursion into philosophy. Bear with me; it will be very short, sketchy and simplistic. I am not a professional philosopher.

Most (quantitative, causal) research and most theories of management or therapy are based on implied **positivism**, which has its roots in **empiricism** and even further back in **realism**: the philosophical position that what we see and experience is real can be discovered and is not subject to being altered by how we think. Through the ages, however, some thinkers have concerned themselves with questions about what 'really' constitutes reality. Some came to the conclusion that we cannot be at all sure about the existence of an 'out-there' reality, only about the ideas in our minds. Plato and others argued, in a metaphysical position updated by Kant, that reality had an essence or **idea** which could only be approximately perceived. This position, **idealism**, can be contrasted with realism. A more specific and psychological kind of idealism is **rationalism**, which is the theory that all knowledge is fundamentally made up of innate rules, which we carry in our minds.

Constructivism is a child of rationalism. It preceded **constructionism** in what was seen as a 'new wave' of therapies and is the idea that we all construct reality in our own minds and thinking. We will not be exploring this philosophy except in noting that we do all construct our own 'take' on reality in our own minds. Much of this book refers to the differences between the different **subjective realities** of different individuals in a group. Carl Rogers (Rogers 1995) brought this phenomenological approach into the field of therapies and was first to consider the interplay of these in relationships. This model is, however, very far from a radical constructivist position, which, like idealism, makes empirical reality unknowable and the 'objective' stance a myth.

Social constructionism is the philosophical base for **Narrative** and **Solution-focused** therapies. In this paradigm, social realities are seen as being **co-constructed** by the persons involved, in interaction with each other, created in dialogue. Most social constructionism, as applied to a therapeutic approach, is not radical. That is, the idea of an independent, objective reality still remains. If we take a table, the physical object is not seen as being socially constructed, but the concept *table* is. Other cultures could potentially construe the same physical object as a chair, a bed, a boat, an ornament. (Of course, the piece of furniture called a table was physically constructed in response to the socially constructed concept!)

Also, real events happen in a real physical universe and are known primarily through the senses (**empiricism**) but the psychological nature of those events is socially constructed.

In the domain of human, especially moral, actions this differentiation can be difficult to make. Rape or murder could be defined as real, objective events and in the sense that they are particular actions or series of actions they are so. We note, however, that they may be determined differently in different cultures. Murder, objectively, is a real action; the wilful killing of another human being. It is universally seen as wrong but killing others in warfare is excepted in most cultures, though not by conscientious objectors. Abortion is not defined as murder by the majority in our time yet a large minority does define it as such.

Does the concept *wilful* or even the concept *murder* itself put murder out of the objective and into the socially constructed domain? Clearly the concept is not a material object or an observable event, yet courts treat it as real, that is, as something which can be objectively discovered. The true–false dichotomy cannot be equated with the objective–constructed dichotomy.

The implications of **relativism** in this take on constructionism are more limited than might be assumed from the statement that reality is socially constructed. We all interact with the world on the basis of assuming that there are absolute non-material truths. Even the concept of true–false is such. To relativists or radical constructionists or constructivists this fundamental **absolutism** is hidden and denied but it is still there. For most social constructionists it creates (or should create) a tension. When can non-material reality be differently co-constructed and when can it not? How relative and modifiable are our concepts? The answers to this tension are different depending on our basic personal philosophies. For example, as a Christian I include in my social constructionist model the idea that both in material and non-material realms that co-creation of reality includes dialogue with a creator God, whose part of the dialogue is absolute truth. C. S. Lewis articulated this position in his essay on the universality of moral judgements (Lewis 1952).

FOR REFLECTION

- Identify how you yourself model reality. Are you more of a realist or idealist, in philosophical terms?
- Apart from the 'out-there' world, how many of your own mental constructs do you believe to be absolutely true?
- Why do you think they have this status?

Social constructionism can be contrasted with **positivism**, in which the concept itself has an objective reality. We often treat our constructs as though they are objectively real. In the last chapter we discussed the concept of process and concepts of human social systems and we treated those concepts as though they had a reality outside the constructions of people trying to understand the world. In Narrative (social constructionist) terms we understand that we could have modelled quite differently.

In positivist terms we take our own constructs as givens. The concept of the transference, for example, is held in the positivist tradition and is seen as having a **real, out-there existence**, which can be discovered, rather than being simply one way of modelling a pattern of interaction. Attachment ideas have also been developed in the positivist tradition, where attachment styles are seen as really existing rather than as being one way of modelling certain patterns of interaction. I must confess to having some attachment to positivism myself and, indeed, I think we all have. As noted above, even the most radical constructivists and social constructionists hold some absolutes, if only the concept of true and false.

Social constructionism, however, reminds us to **hold our 'truths' lightly and consider whether they could be alternatively constructed in a different culture or different paradigm**. As we can see, we all have a tendency to reify our constructs. This particularly happens

with constructs which are accepted by a large part of our group, especially when that group itself is large, such as a particular culture. The
problem with this is that every way of modelling can preclude another
way of modelling. Our reality is not only constructed in this way; it is
also so constrained. Seeing an object as a table might blind one to its
other potential functions.

Life as story: deconstructing the problem plot and co-creating the preferred outcome

Through Social Constructionism we might view our lives as stories;
stories which we co-create in interaction with other people and with
events. This ongoing, ever-changing narration is not only one of words.
Badenoch and Cox (in Gantt & Badenoch 2013) point out that we begin
forming embodied memories as infants, before we develop language,
and that these implicit memories act as a filter during our subsequent
lives. While we are using words to communicate we are also engaged
in an ongoing meta communication made up of 'body language', vocal
tone and so on. (Watzlawick et al. 2011). These authors point out that
the non-verbal is an essential part of the communication; the 'how to
read' message which accompanies the words. We all engage in an ongoing stream of this meta-communication. Some of our non-verbal communication seems to be hard-wired. Matsumoto et al. (2013) point out
that the recognition of facial expressions of seven basic emotions (joy,
fear surprise, anger, disgust, sadness and contempt) is cross-cultural and
that the expressions conveying these emotions are produced even by
those who are congenitally blind.

Epston and White (1990) proposed the application of the concepts
of **dominant** and **alternative knowledges.** The dominant knowledge is
the consensus of the group and there is considerable pressure for group
members to conform to this way of thinking (Brown 2000).

*The team behind the one-way mirror were becoming very irritated with the
woman in the therapy room. As the therapist was interviewing the couple
about their management of their children, the father seemed sensible and
democratic and the mother autocratic and even abusive in her attempts
at discipline. There was a picture building up of her as a monster mother.*

*When the therapist came out for a break, revealing the same judgement
of the couple as the team was holding, it seemed that the team would
reinforce her thinking. However, the supervisor pointed out that 'systemic
neutrality' had been lost and asked the therapist to go in and interview*

the woman as empathically as possible, as though she were an individual client, trying to get only her point of view.

A huge change happened in the rest of the session. The woman spoke movingly of her lack of support, of the way her husband left all disciplining responsibility to her while being able to come in as a 'Father Christmas' parent. The team were now able to see her vulnerability and the necessity for her husband to give her more backup and take more responsibility. When this later happened the mother became less rigid and authoritarian, the self-esteem and self-efficacy of both parents improved and the situation of the children in the family became much healthier.

In this vignette we see an example of a **dominant knowledge**; that held by both team and therapist in response to the conversation in the therapy room and the narrative which was beginning to develop there. Fortunately, the supervisor held at least the possibility of an **alternative knowledge** and directed the therapist in a course which **reconstructed** the **problem plot** (White 2007). The new story which developed took the family out of a crystallised, stuck position and made change possible. This vignette is also an example of a team losing, but then regaining, systemic neutrality (see discussion in the last chapter). What seemed obvious in the pattern being viewed (positivist position) proved rather different when the alternative knowledge was applied.

If the supervisor had held the same view as the team and therapist this reconstruction of the problem narrative might not have occurred and the family might well have stayed stuck. Fortunately, the supervisor had the power to invoke a change of story. If the alternative knowledge had been held by a junior member of the team, that member might not have had enough power to institute the change of direction. On the other hand, the therapist, if given enough reflective space and a theory which encouraged her to challenge negative stories she might be holding, might have been able to change direction herself; if not in this session then in a later one. Of course, the experience of this session might have been so aversive to the mother that she might have refused to come back for a later one – thus reinforcing the view of her as a rigid and impossible person!

The narrative critique

Unfortunately, the loosening of the one version of reality illustrated in the above example often does not occur in general life, where the dominant plot attains a truth status, excluding the possibility of another truth. This can happen in our own individual realities, where we see our own point of view as being absolutely correct and therefore any other version of reality as false or at best misguided. The effect becomes even more powerful and problematic when the dominant story is held by a group, or a majority within a group. The constraining power of a dominant belief allows little space to generate any alternative.

Let us consider one important dominant paradigm, in the field of mental health, where the ways of thinking in our society are still based on the positivist medical model.

Early ideas about human problems (psychopathology) were modelled on a medical praxis which had proved very useful. A man has a fever. You determine that it is caused by a bacterial infection. Deal with the infection by killing the bacteria. The man is cured.

As we remember from the last chapter, this is an example of linear causality. A causes B; deal with A and you can cure B. Early ideas about resolving psychological problems focused on the problem and its hypothesised cause. But even if it were possible to identify such a cause, because that cause is in the past it cannot be altered directly in the present; the bacterium is still present to be killed but an attachment trauma in early childhood is an historical event, no longer available for direct counteraction.

Watzlawick et al. (2011, p. 139) point out that in most human histories, 'the past is not available except as reported in the present and therefore is not pure content but has a relationship aspect as well'. The apparent linear causal chain is extremely complex and circular, with the present co-constructing of the story influencing even the memory, which is being constructed in the present (Davies & Dalgleish 2001).

Modern approaches, both in management and therapy, emphasise focusing on current problems and how to mend them. One downside to this approach is that **focusing on problems can increase the salience of negative stories and paradoxically make positive outcomes harder to achieve.**

In the post-modern, social constructionist approach, practitioners are very mindful of this effect and seek rather to **deconstruct** the problem story by focusing on 'not-problem' or exceptions and then encouraging the development of a history of these more positive alternatives. This does not mean that problems are ignored in some fuzzy 'positive thinking' modus. They can, indeed, be ignored by Solution-focused practitioners, who work purely with the **Miracle Question** and the extent to which it is in place; though Solution-focused practitioners will also listen empathically to an account of problems if clients really feel a need to recount them. The advocates of the Solution-focused approach, Steve de Shazar, his wife, Insoo Kim Berg, and their associates were the first to point out the effect of **looking for exceptions** in reducing or eliminating problems (e.g. De Shazar & Dolan 2007). They introduced the idea of amplifying exceptions to the problem plot rather than focusing on the problem plot itself.

Exceptions and the 'flip side'

Social Constructionist approaches, rather than looking back at the problem and its patterns, tend to look forward to the **preferred future** and its patterns (Eron & Lund 1996). This Solution-focused model has been taken up not only in the therapy world but very much in the thinking of organisational consultants (Bunker & Alban 1997). This is the outcome or solution that clients themselves want. There is then exploration of what of the preferred outcome already exists, focusing particularly on exceptions to the **problem plot**. This practice, in Narrative work, is very like the Solution-focused use of the Miracle Question with rating scales to determine how much of the miracle is already in place (De Shazar & Dolan 2007). Organisations do this by starting with a Mission Statement and then mapping what is already in place to get there and a plan for achieving what is not. (This practice also includes the use of values, which we will discuss further below.)

*In the Eating Disorders (ED) group (Group 2, Chapter 2), immediately after the introductory exercises all participants were given paper and an envelope with their name on it. They were asked to think about how they wanted things to be by the end of the course and write this on the paper, which was then sealed in the envelope and kept by the facilitators until the final session, when they got their own envelopes back to read for themselves. The task was **not** framed as 'your goals' or 'your aims', as these labels are potentially constraining, implying a deficit model: 'I have to achieve something I have not yet achieved', 'I have to get somewhere and I'm not there yet'. They are also **internalising** (see below), implying that all the change has to be within or about the individual.*

Giving the task very near the beginning of the group helped to set the process and introduce some implicit rules. The focus was to be around a preferred outcome in the future, framed however the individual wanted to frame it. What felt too personal would not need to be shared; facilitators emphasised that the notes on the paper were for each individual and would not be read by anyone else.

The task was also useful in the last session, when participants opened and read their own notes and could choose whether or not to share with the group what was written and how much of what was desired was now present. It therefore made an important contribution to evaluation and closing.

While ideas about using exceptions and a **preferred future** were taking root in the field of therapy, in the perspective of dealing with very large groups (organisations and communities), Lippett and his colleagues, notably Schindler-Rainman and Dannemiller (Bunker & Alban 1997), also began to develop group activities and ideas around a **preferred future**. They worked with as many as a thousand people together at one time.

FOR REFLECTION

- Reflect on something you currently see as a problem in your own life.
- When does the problem not happen?
- How will things be when your preferred future is in place around this issue?
- How much of the preferred future is already in place?
- How do you take one more small step towards that future?

Scaffolding, content and kinds of question

In the example above, not only do we illustrate the use of the preferred future (outcome) but note that the nature of that outcome is generated entirely by the participant/s. One important characteristic of Narrative (and Solution-focused) work is that the **content** is supplied by clients rather than therapists/facilitators. This is in contrast with, for example, a CBT approach, where there is a commitment to collaboration but more assumption that the **therapist takes an expert teacher position**. Solutions are known and furnished by experts. In Narrative work the assumption is that clients can generate solutions out of their own unique experiences and skill sets if therapists provide the right **scaffolding** (White 2007). Scaffolding is the name White gives to the sets of questions designed to **elicit the client's own memories which construct the alternative knowledge or preferred outcome.**

Supplying the right scaffolding is by no means simple; White is highly prescriptive about the questions to be asked and the order of asking them. There are three major themes of questioning which create this Narrative 'scaffolding': **externalising**, use of **landscapes** to connect up the **alternative plot** and **re-membering/outsider witnessing/definitional ceremony.**

Although some Narrative practitioners might not use White's scaffolding, the principle of most of the content being generated by the clients/group participants is fundamental to the approach and its philosophical base. It is essential to uncover the knowledges of every mind in the group to provide a richness of possible solution or task achievement.

For this reason, relatively **open questions** are used preferentially by the facilitator. A **closed question** is one which limits the domain of the answer; the ultimate is a question which demands a 'yes' or 'no' reply. 'What is your name?' is another example of a closed question. Some questions are a little wider than this; for example, 'What themes do you notice?' There is really a continuum between more closed and more open questions, depending on what is needed in the conversation. 'Tell me more about that', is an open question which still limits the answer a bit; 'that' is the referent and one would not expect a comment which had no relationship with the subject at hand.

Closed questions do have their own usefulness. They are less anxiety-provoking than open questions and are often employed at the beginning of a session to put participants more at ease. They cannot, however, open a space for new or forgotten knowledge; they keep the answer within the questioner's frame of reference.

After a relatively open question is asked there is likely to be a short silence. This is because the answer is not immediately obvious and therefore **this silence is to be desired** in any Narrative work. Usually the knowledge for the **problem (thin) plot** is over-rehearsed and easily accessed. Some research indicates also that we are neurologically primed to notice negatives and problems more than we notice positives (Smith et al. 2003). The **alternative knowledge**, that which needs to be accessed for the development of the **preferred future**, is more difficult to access, so the person being asked will have to think for a while to generate the answer. In fact, there is often an immediate answer, 'I don't know,' and it is tempting to move on in the conversation. A good

Narrative practitioner slows down, **waiting for and even re-prompting an answer to this alternative knowledge question**.

Radical listening and deconstructing

Weingarten (1998) proposed that an essential skill in a Narrative approach is that of **radical listening**. When we listen to others our heads are very busy making our own constructions of them and their information. This can apply particularly to therapists, doctors and similar professionals, who are trained to diagnose pathology, formulate, develop hypotheses. If we are too occupied with these tasks our constructing interferes seriously with our being able to hear what the other is trying to tell us.

Weingarten proposes that we should avoid all these cognitive exercises and instead try to become experience-near; to focus our efforts on attempting to understand as completely as possible the experiences being described and the meanings that person is trying to convey. This **radical listening** is an essential skill for a facilitator. We can never be sure that we are really understanding others but the more we understand that we don't understand the less 'noise' interferes. All of our curiosity is poured into relating, an intense focus on our interlocutors and the meanings they are trying to convey. In turn, their experience is of being better heard than usual. Of people who do radical listening it is often said, 'They get it!'.

This communication gap between us, the 'understanding that we don't understand', can be modelled as the 'interference' in any transmitted message. Sometimes the interference is worse than at other times. Generally, the closer we are in culture, whether macro-culture, family culture or professional culture, the more likely it is that our meanings will closely approximate each other. As a heuristic of social intercourse we tend to assume that others do understand what we mean and that we understand them. This is not necessarily so. If I say I am depressed you might believe that you know what I mean but actually we might have mental constructions which are very different. (In some cultures the word itself does not exist, so there is no 'depression' meaning.)

This difference might give rise to important and unseen misunderstandings and indeed can be a source of conflict with both of us assuming 'bad faith' of the other. The clash between what I think is obvious and what you think is obvious could make both of us believe the other to be disingenuous or dishonest. This can particularly happen the more different we are as individuals. In different cultures, genders, professions and even families, with different life experiences, we have very diverse **subjective realities.**

It is therefore part of a facilitator's work to seek clarity of meaning and to be curious about how messages are received. In radical listening, part of this is achieved by **deconstructing**: asking detailed questions about what is being conveyed. The richer the description the better hearers can understand the experiences being conveyed and also the more chance there is of co-constructing a preferred outcome. Deconstructing questions are those which do not assume that everyone has the same subjective reality. They go deeper and deeper into what meaning the speaker is really trying to convey. In doing so they might change the perceptions of both speaker and hearers. It is usually important after asking a deconstructing question to leave a pause for the other person to access information which is not readily available because of the subjective feeling, 'That's just how it is.'

One way to ask deconstructing questions is to pick up on rhetorical questions and turn them into real questions. Here is an example:

Alec: *Why do I put up with her behaviour?*
James: *(in a curious, rather than affirming or disconfirming tone) Good point. Why do you put up with her behaviour?*

I have another favourite kind of deconstructing questioning, which I call the 'string of why's'. This reaches into a deeper and deeper sense of what is happening. Here is an example:

Jenny: *It makes me really upset when Jon walks in here all grouchy!*
Bob: *I wonder, why is that?*
Jenny: *Well, it's upsetting when someone is grouchy!*
Bob: *Yes, I get that, and I guess we all get a bit upset if someone is grouchy. But it seems really to get to you, and particularly if it is Jon. I wonder why?*
Jenny: *(after a pause) I think it reminds me of when my dad came home in a bad mood and we would all get very tense. It was as though we were just waiting for some doom to fall on us.*

An essential part of radical listening is what White calls **catharsis**, using the word in its Greek drama meaning, not its modern meaning; to instil a change or movement. It is all very well to listen to what people say. Complimenting them on their input is a frequent social manoeuvre but can be insincere and we often disregard compliments made to us as having little validity. The real test of whether you have been listening to me and really appreciate what I contribute is if it impacts on you and changes what you do or think. It is important to set up a culture in a group in which people specifically acknowledge each other's ideas. Ideally, they will also **feed back how those ideas have changed their thinking or actions**. See more about this in the section on Outsider Witnessing, later in this chapter.

FOR REFLECTION

- Do you tell people when their words have moved you to a positive difference of thinking or action?
- Try listening to someone with no agenda but to understand as vividly as possible what experience they are telling you about.
- When you hear a rhetorical question try being curious and turning it into a real question. What happens?
- Try using a series of why's. Do you get to a deeper level of description?

Externalising

A favourite saying for Systemic and Narrative theorists is, '**The person is not the problem; the problem is the problem.**' White (2007) points out that we have not only a positivist view of problems but also a habit of **internalising discourse**, making those problems an integral part of a person's identity. We speak of people as being 'a psychopath', 'a schizophrenic', 'a depressive', 'an alcoholic'. The person becomes the problem. This internalising of labels attaches the problem to the person's identity with an implication of permanence.

When our personhood is under attack we instinctively defend. If I am 'an alcoholic' I need to defend drinking behaviour.

White and Epston suggested that we should change to **externalising** discourse, viewing the problem as a character in the person's story; a character who influences me and those around me and can also be influenced by us.

So I am not 'depressive'; I have Depression in my life. What metaphor do I use to describe Depression? Is it a dark cloud? If so, what happens to me and my family and friends when it settles, when it becomes lighter or lifts? What might we all notice that we do which encourages it to settle or lift? Or is it a Black Dog? When does it get bigger or smaller? Can it be house trained, lead trained? How do I and others get it to behave differently, to grow smaller and tamer? What does it do which disadvantages or advantages my life?

In externalising we can get a different relationship with the problem. Since it is not integral to our identity we are free to consider it more objectively and we are empowered to change our relationship with it and its influence on us. It might not be a matter of getting rid of it. In externalising conversation it is important to map both positive and negative effects.

The negative influence of the problem	On me	On my partner	On my family	On my friends
The positive influence of the problem	On me	On my partner	On my family	On my friends
Making the problem more the way I want it	What I do	What my partner does	What my family does	What my friends do
Making the problem worse	What I do	What my partner does	What my family does	What my friends do

Table 3.1 Mapping the problem in externalising

Epston and White (1990) discovered the use of externalising originally in their work with children, and certainly children can engage very easily in the process. A group of children of about 5 – 7 years old, asked to 'draw a portrait of your Sadness', for example, will set to with no hesitation; adults will typically consider the request bizarre. Adults will, however, usually externalise around a diagnostic or problem label. In groups, as we will see later (e.g. conflict resolution in Chapter 5) one can use terms like 'the dance' or 'the vicious circle' as characters to externalise. It is interesting that as long as the therapists or facilitators have themselves a mental picture of the 'out there' problem, most of those they speak to will automatically also begin to externalise, usually well within one hour of the conversation start. Some professionals are the exceptions to this; they have been too well indoctrinated in internalising discourse.

White (2007) emphasises that very adversarial or totalising metaphors are not necessarily helpful for externalising because of the greater anxiety aroused by a battle concept and because they could have the paradoxical effect of making clients feel more disempowered and even more of a failure if they could not completely eliminate the problem. He said that, nevertheless, if an adversarial metaphor first springs to mind we can go along with that until another presents – we don't have to be rigid or stick to the same 'characters' when we externalise. The following example shows a shift from an adversarial to another, less totalising externalisation.

In the second session of the ED Group (Group 2, chapter 2) participants are asked to 'write a letter to your friend, the Food Gremlin and another letter to your enemy, the Food Gremlin'. 'Food Gremlin' is the name this particular group developed to cover all the varied ED's presenting in the group. (It is possibly not the best metaphor, since it contains the word 'food' but it is adequate for this point of the process.) This exercise is designed to begin the positive and negative mapping of the externalised ED. Interestingly, where the Food Gremlin took the form of Bulimia participants could do the 'enemy' letter easily but found the 'friend' one very difficult; where the Gremlin took the form of Anorexia the 'friend' letter was easy and the 'enemy' one very difficult. (An internalising description of this effect would be that Bulimia is ego-dystonic and Anorexia ego-syntonic!) The contents of the letters then formed a basis for a very fruitful discussion. Similarities in what the Food Gremlin was saying to each of them in terms of their identities had already been visited in the first session.

For the following session they were asked to bring a portrait of their Gremlin, made up however they liked, by drawing, painting, collage or any other form. Lisa brought two collage pictures; one of a very sweet, friendly little green character and one of red, demonic, staring eyes. This was a breakthrough in her being able to see the 'enemy' aspect of her Gremlin and her task became to turn the 'eyes', which bullied and abused her, back to the friendly little green Gremlin. At this time the group learned that Lisa collected soft toys and this gave later opportunities for them to help her around grounding and self-soothing.

Landscaping and values

White was very struck with Bruner's concept of two **landscapes**, that of consciousness and that of action, or events. We all experience certain events but then we act upon that raw data cognitively, the landscape of consciousness. Problems can arise out of events, such as a traumatic assault, but what makes them ongoing problems is how we subsequently deal with them in our own minds. Our dealing with them often follows patterns which we developed early in our lives (see Chapter 2). Sometimes these patterns work well but often they do not.

All the patterns, whether positive or negative in effect, are made up of both actions (events) and cognitions, so involve moving between these two landscapes. In narrative work a history is built up by moving backwards and forwards in time and from one landscape to another. This might be a history of the problem but is more likely to be the building up of a preferred outcome history by tracing exceptions to the problem, also known as **unique outcomes** or **sparkling moments** (White & Epston 1990).

In White's later work he had become fascinated with trauma and the use of **values** to re-establish a secure personal identity. Values have the advantage of having only a positive valence. We can have negative schemas about ourselves ('I am evil', 'I am unkind') but the values involved are always positive ('goodness is important', 'kindness is important'). Increasingly, the history being mapped on the two landscapes became a history or the playing out of personal values.

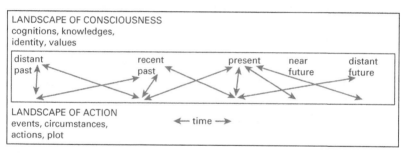

Figure 3.1 Landscaping

Source: After White (2007)

Jane: *I feel so terrible about how I was this morning! I really lost it!*
Maggie: *Why, what happened?*
Jane: *Well, my mother was dithering around as usual. Remember, I told you that she has the beginnings of dementia, so it's really not her fault. I was running late and I shouted at her and told her she was an old nuisance! I don't know how I'm going to manage things as she gets older and worse! (Jane becomes tearful in reporting this – a clear indication that a central value has been involved).*
Maggie: *What does that mean about what is important to you?*
Jane: *Why ... what?*
Maggie: *Why do you feel SO bad for shouting at her and telling her she was a nuisance?*
Jane: *Well, it's obvious! It's just so unkind to do that!*
Maggie: *So it's important to be kind?*

Jane: *Of course!*

Maggie: *Can you remember any very early incident which shows how important kindness is to you?*

Jane: *(After a reflective pause) Well, I can't remember a particular incident but I do remember that I used to be very worried when the younger children were upset and I would take them to my special hidey-hole in the hedge and read them stories or do a pretend tea party to cheer them up.*

Maggie: *Anything more recent?*

Jane: *(Another pause) I remember at high school there was a girl who was bullied quite a lot because she wasn't as well off as the rest of us and was often dressed in passed-down clothes. I befriended her and made sure she spent time at home with me and was always invited when I had a party or anything. Eventually the bullies gave up on her ... We stayed friends right through college, until she moved away and then we sort of lost touch ...*

Maggie: *What about ... last week, say?*

Jane: *What about last week?*

Maggie: *Can you think of anything that happened last week which shows how important kindness is to you?*

Jane: *(Thinks for a while again) Well, I suppose I was quite busy helping the new girl at work to get her head round the systems – they never give much support to the newies!*

(Later in the conversation ...)

Maggie: *Given how important kindness is to you, how well do you think you will manage your mother's ongoing deterioration?*

Jane: *Oh, I know I shall often get impatient, but I'll go on looking after her and when she needs more care I'll make really sure she gets the right facility or services! Maybe I should start researching that now?...*

In the above discussion Jennie is **landscaping** Jane's own discovered value of kindness. By the end of the conversation Jane has a strong sense of herself as a kind person. This is in contrast with the beginning, where she sees herself as unkind. From a feeling of defeat she moves to being able to think about the future with her aging mother with some positivity. **Because she has defined herself as fundamentally a kind person, she is even more likely to engage in kind rather than unkind behaviours.** A negative **problem plot** is turning into the alternative **preferred future** (Eron & Lund 1996).

White and his colleagues developed this technique largely in work with individuals. In a group, the facilitator can have such a conversation in a basically dyadic way and this will still impact on the rest of the group. In Chapter 6 Tom Smiley describes how he sometimes does this as part of working with an inpatient group on a Mental Health unit. I have used it also in pairs or had the landscaping conversation with the whole group as a series of 'resonances'.

> **Ruth (Supervisor):** *Jill, when you spoke of how difficult it was to decide not to offer therapy to that client, I wonder why that was?*
>
> **Jill:** *Well, I knew she didn't fit our service but I don't think she is going to get a suitable service and she really needs help and support. Her life's a mess!*
>
> **Ruth:** *So what does that mean about what is important to you?*
>
> **Jill:** *I guess I'm in this job because I want to help people. Kindness and making them able to have happy lives – that's important!*
>
> **Ruth:** *Is this making the rest of you also remember times when you felt deeply grieved because of not being able to help someone?*
>
> **Helen:** *(After a short pause) Yes, it seems to happen so often. There are so many people who need therapy support and the therapy resources in our service are so limited. I feel as though I am having to send people away all the time … And yes, I agree with Jill. We are in this job because we want to help those people.*
>
> **Jim:** *For me, it's when I have to terminate because we have reached the end of our ten sessions. That's okay if the client has met the goals but not if there seems to be lots more to do. Remember, when I talked about that case last time, and we discussed what I could suggest, because I was quite sure that there was complex trauma, but we couldn't continue. I always find those situations hard.*
>
> **Ruth:** *So I guess you all have to reflect on how you personally can help as many people as possible, because that's important to you. And come to terms with the fact that you can't help them all.*
>
> **Julie:** *Yes, that's what I try to remember. There are so many people out there who need help but at least we can be happy about the ones we do manage to give tools to change their lives for the better.*
>
> **Ruth:** *Who remembers an early incident which shows that helping people is important to you?*

If Ruth wants to track this any further she can draw out a future orientation of what it means to the team/service that they are all so passionate about helping people. She might also divert into looking at the pressures engendered by that value and how they could honour the value while not being tempted into burnout or broken boundaries.

Clashes of values, and which ones are being evoked, can cause passionate disagreement and even conflict in groups and it is well for the facilitator to be aware of the possible pressures which make members react emotionally. White (2004) says that where there is strong emotion or even trauma it is because a dearly held value seems to be under attack.

Brian and Dan are both dedicated Christians and leaders in their church. They disagree vehemently on the subject of whether Christians, saved by grace and the redeeming work of Christ, can ever lose their salvation. (The issue has nuances which are often disputed by sincere and learned Bible scholars; neither position can be shown to be absolutely 'the truth'.)

Brian believes that Christians can never lose their salvation and passionately wants to convey this to the congregation. Earlier in his life he went through a period of intense self-criticism and discouragement, feeling he was not a 'good enough' Christian. The doctrine that the elect remain the elect, whatever their shortcomings, burst into his life like a light and rescued him from this depression. He has since been an active and fruitful Christian. David supports Brian because he reasons that since God is foreknowing He can also decide in advance who is and who isn't saved.

Dan, on the other hand, had a brother who, believing that he was saved whatever his actions, entered into an adulterous relationship which caused destructive family processes. He drifted progressively away from the church and declared himself an atheist by the end of his life. Dan therefore thinks that the 'once saved always saved' doctrine can lead people to think that all behaviours are permissible and ultimately take them away from God. Gemma agrees with Dan's position because she feels that it would be unfair for God to decide in advance who will be saved, and God can't be unfair.

A good facilitator will notice and convey that both men are intensely committed to the value of Christians remaining faithful, fruitful and joyful. This is a key joint value. The difference in their life experiences makes them genuinely inclined to different positions on the issue. David and Gemma similarly are motivated by important values, even though these lead them to different conclusions. Noting this can make them all able to leave space for the other's convictions and live in harmony, in spite of their disagreements.

In this example both men show strong emotionality about their positions because the underlying values are so important to them. This effect underlies most serious conflict. It is necessary to:

1. Assume that both protagonists are coming from genuinely held beliefs and values. This **assumption of good faith** is very important in groups or dyads. We tend to assume of those who disagree with us that they are either stupid or lying. In other words, we make an

assumption of **bad** faith. This effect is especially salient in couple conflict.

2. We need to be curious about the background to the emotion shown. If, instead of making hasty assumptions of bad faith, we keep a calm curiosity about what is valued so much and why, we are better able to understand and respect that person.

3. The facilitative task is to find the underlying area of agreement; the value which unites the protagonists.

We all have implicit values which underlie our arguments. One way in which clashes might occur is in the fact that different individuals might have different values being threatened on certain occasions. Our cultures and life experiences might give us very idiosyncratic ways of detecting threats to our value system. On the other hand, central values are universal and even apply across cultures. An important task of a good facilitator is to hold up a mirror in which members can see their commonality of value. Different cultures may have different ways of playing out these values but there is a basis for profound agreement. We all want kindness, honesty, justice, commitment. Even when we are mocking these things we are demonstrating how important they are to us and we are likely to become indignant if they are not displayed towards us.

FOR REFLECTION

-   Think of a time you disagreed strongly with someone.
-   Identify which of your values was activated (what was important to you that underlay your strong opinion).
-   What value do you think the other person might have been defending (use the assumption of good faith)?
-   Would there be a way to agree, based on values you both had in common?

The more a group has a sense of shared values, the more positive its dynamics. Organisations like to start decision-making processes with a 'vision' based on values, or a preferred future in which those values are played out (Bunker & Alban 1997). This **drawing together of members around shared values is something we see as fundamental to any good group process**. As in the above example, different values might be elicited in different arguments because of circumstances or personal histories, but the likelihood is that the protagonists share an important foundation of strongly held values. Getting to this foundation allows an increasing diversity of opinions.

Re-membering, re-telling and outsider witnessing

To decide what is 'really true' we often depend on witnessing from outside ourselves. As we discussed previously, we develop the plots of our life narrative in interaction with others. If we had the misfortune to be abused or heavily criticised while we were young, or if we interpreted some input negatively, we might have a 'thin' problematic plot. But there were other voices in our lived experience; people who appreciated us and could expand our potential. Because of that tendency, which we have noted, of selectively remembering the negative more easily than the positive and because we remember best what fits the dominant knowledge, we don't easily access those voices. However, they can be accessed. Just as landscaping is used to find a history of value-imbued events so it can also **bring into the conversation those silenced voices**. Sometimes the voices are of people who are no longer in touch or even alive; this is not important. Here are some **re-membering** questions:

> *What would your grandfather say about your having learned to do that?*
> *Who was most likely to notice that you were courageous enough to do this?*
> *What was it about you that made your friend's mother want your influence on her daughter?*
> *What made you love your nan so much? What was it about her? What was it about you that made her love you so much?*

The latter two kinds of questions are particularly important in healing a crippled sense of identity. Some people can see how others have had a good influence on them but are unable to see that they had a good influence on others or were valued by them. Those lost voices are re-evoked and amplified as witness to the more positive story.

In the use of outsider witnessing, the witness has the same function. In this case the witness, rather than being someone remembered, is a current hearer of the story. In a group the whole group acts as outsider witness.

White (2007) describes the use of outsider witnessing in individual work and has very prescribed stages of **scaffolding** questions. The outsider witness is typically a non-professional volunteer who has had similar experiences to the client and the therapist is to scaffold by asking the witness the following, after the client has recounted the story:

1. *What words did X say which particularly struck you?*
2. *What did this make you think about X?*
3. *What images came into your head?*
4. *How did those images resonate with things in your life?*
5. *How do you think this might make you do things differently in the future?*
6. (In a later session, if this becomes possible – White calls this **extended catharsis**) *How did what X said change what you did yourself in your own life?*

The scaffolding can be extended (after #5) by asking the client a similar set of questions about what the witness said, thus entering into a telling and re-telling process.

I have found in my own practice that it can be very complicated to set up outsider witnessing in its pure Whitean form, so the technique has limited usefulness. The principles, however, are useful and particularly so in working with groups. Typically, I will keep the structure much looser and in fact may not get past the first question; *What about what X said resonates with any of you?* I then wait for responses. If necessary I might follow up with some of the other questions but generally the bouncing around the room of resonances deepens group cohesion and positive identity development, both for group and individuals. Remember, from Chapter 1, that we define our own identities largely in the context of the groups to which we belong and their perceived value, as well as our own perceived value in them.

Writings and ceremonies

Another way to increase the witnessing, and therefore the power, of co-creating the preferred outcome is for the alternative story to be supported by written materials. These could be letters, certificates, or even, in these times, emails and texts. David Epston particularly developed the use of writing in Narrative work.

Here is an example of a letter from a supervisor to a group of mental health professionals.

Dear team,

I found yesterday's supervision session as stimulating as usual and am always grateful for what I learn from you – even though I am the supervisor! An example of this yesterday was Joel's description of an excellent piece of inter-agency work. I too shall be bearing in mind that principle of analysing which layer of management has the executive power to make a particular change happen.

I am noticing that you are more and more able as a team to talk about difficult interactions. I admired your courage, Brenda, in raising the subject of your occasional feeling of rejection when the others in the open plan space are too busy to greet you. It was interesting that whereas in times past the team would have rushed in with 'polite' reassurance, on this occasion you were all able to reflect about how one could signal, at the same time, acceptance of the other and busyness which requires full focus. I liked the creativity of some of your ideas, like the 'must concentrate' sign. Joan, you are usually very quiet but when you do share your reflections, as you did on the rising levels of personal expectations in the team, you really seem to hit the nail on the head and express something which resonates for all the others.

I wonder where you would now plot yourselves on that line of becoming the team you would all prefer? How have you managed to move in your preferred direction? It might be good for us to use part of our next session to think about the practices which are making you all more confident and supported. What effects do these changes make on your clinical efficacy?

Written input like the above is designed to continue the development of a preferred narrative and outplaying of change between sessions. The questions are designed to help participants continue to reflect on what is working and how that can be enhanced.

Specific and concrete examples are important. Narrative work eschews vague and meaningless compliments, which are discounted by recipients, just as standard social reassurance would have had less impact than the reflective addressing of the problem as described in this example. Instead, specifics are mentioned and linked to their usefulness. The comment on Joe's account is an example of what White (2007) calls **catharsis**. This is evidence that the account has made a difference in the life or practice of the hearer.

Notice also the support given in particular to two people whose need for that support might be greater than the needs of the others in the group. Brenda had done something socially dangerous, but important in really successful group process, by exposing her own vulnerability. The response, both by the group and by the supervisor, makes this kind of communication safer in the future. Joan is one of those group members who are comparatively silent. It is essential to amplify the positive impact of her input so that she can feel more confident to share her ideas in sessions.

Summary: the essence of a narrative approach

We are constantly co-creating ourselves in relationship with others and with the events of our lives. We all have our own subjective realities and we tend to consider our own ideas and opinions to be the truth. This can crowd out space for other people's truths and at worst leads to antagonism and an assumption that the other is either stupid or lying. We often give a reality to our own opinions and constructs. In a group these differences need to be acknowledged and celebrated rather than being allowed to create conflict. It is very important for facilitators to model and promote radical listening; curiosity and acceptance of different and even conflicting experiences and viewpoints.

Negative ideas, whether about ourselves, others or the world, seem often to have greater salience than positive ideas. It has been suggested that we are hard-wired to notice negatives rather than positives because it is necessary to be alert to threats to our wellbeing. Unfortunately, this very negativity often forms a dominant, problem, 'thin' plot. A narrative approach seeks to add unconsidered alternative knowledges to thicken the plot and make space for change in the direction of preferred outcomes. Whether in groups or individuals, this adds information and potential for creativity. Focus on negatives can increase their dominance. Focusing on exceptions and not-problems, including personal values, co-discovering a history for these, makes for positive change. Ways to loosen the identity or relational network from negative stuckness include having externalising conversations, affirming by outsider witnessing and re-introducing forgotten, affirming voices through re-membering.

FOR REFLECTION

- If possible, try out/roleplay these techniques and ideas with colleagues or friends.
- Notice what sort of input from others helps you to mature and solve problems.
- Think about people who have been positive and caring to you in your life and ask yourself what it was that made them value you.

4

GROUP DEVELOPMENT OVER TIME: SETTING THE CULTURE AND DEEPENING ENGAGEMENT

Here we consider group development over time for short-term and long-term groups. We differentiate between closed and open (and semi-open) groups and look at issues of new membership in long-term groups. We look in detail at how to set the implicit ground rules, which are even more important than those which are made explicit, in order to optimise group culture. Taking a developmental approach, we consider ideas and techniques for starting a group or re-starting one in which the process has become dysfunctional. I have used these ideas both for new groups and for existing teams; especially those referred to me because they have serious interpersonal problems. In the latter case the process of culture setting might have to be slower over time. For new groups it can happen in the first session.

Preparing to start a group

Maybe we should start before the group begins. Obviously if a group is being formed it is important to plan it conceptually. How big will it be? What is the purpose? Will it be a closed or an open group? How long will it exist; is it planned to continue indefinitely or for a certain number of sessions? The purpose for which a group is being formed is the obvious starting point and will determine many of the other variables.

1. SIZE
Work teams have specific areas of operation in the context of the organisation as a whole. Their size will be decided by a computation of the varieties of skills required, the man-hours of each necessary to achieve

objectives and the economic constraints in place. The optimal size of the group will be driven more by task requirements than by psycho-social theorising.

For education, the tension is between economies, which dictate the largest possible group size per instructor/facilitator, and efficacy, which can demand a small group. In fact, one-to-one tuition is best in some situations. I did find, however, when I was engaged in private tuition, that one-to-one might be too intense and a group size of two to five was better, giving space for each pupil to do some individual work without concern about the teacher's gaze. There is also more opportunity for the cross-fertilisation of ideas.

In fact **group size dictates intensity of relationship and felt safety**. Dyads (groups of two) are most intimate but can be too intense. They are stabilised by adding a third (see Chapter 2). To break down the sense of strangeness and social anxiety in a group of strangers, inviting early interaction in dyads loosens the dynamic most efficiently. Generally, the smaller the group, the less social anxiety is engendered. Therapeutic groups are usually limited to a maximum of about eight participants, unless they are more instructional and less reliant on interpersonal dynamics. I have found, however, that bigger therapeutic groups can be constructed, as long as they are frequently broken up for interaction in smaller group-ings. I tend to use the '2–5 members' formula for these subgroups; this is a size which enables everyone to make a contribution of ideas. Varying the membership of the subgroups helps to keep the whole larger group unified.

In small group work, participants themselves sometimes form into bigger groups than five. In contrast to what I have said above, they find this more comfortable because you can hide in a bigger group and just keep silent. I never allow this; always insist that the small work-ing group should split into two if it gets to six or more individuals. To allow larger groups means that you tacitly set up a culture in which some participate and some do not. This interferes with the principle of making all knowledges available and of developing a real and relatively schism-free intimacy among group members.

FOR REFLECTION

- In what size of group are you likely to voice your own opinions?
- What does this mean about your relative confidence?
- Thinking about a group you belong to, how well do you know the other members and their personal opinions? Why is it like this?

2.   ASSESSING FOR MEMBERSHIP: WHAT IS WHOSE BUSINESS?

Obviously, when people join teams they will have been selected for their posts on the basis of their skill sets. Similarly, for focus groups, we need to decide what areas of expertise and experience should be included and find those participants who best meet these criteria. Decision-making groups will include those who represent the various interests involved (stakeholders) in coming to the required decision. In all of these groups the task dictates who the members will be. The selecting organisation/ authority has the responsibility to deliver on its objectives. It is therefore the business of that organisation to do the selecting.

In the field of education, by contrast, participants generally select themselves or are selected or proposed for selection by their parents or guardians. Some selection might then be undertaken by the facility offering the teaching or training. As with work groups, if such selection takes place it is usually focused on competence to achieve the course goals. This, of course, involves some prediction and guesswork. Someone who meets the competency baseline, for example by passing a particular examination, might prove not to be able to do the course after all, for various reasons. (Of course this also applies to those employed for a task.)

Here the participant self-selects because of wanting to learn what is being offered. Selection is the participant's business. However, it can also be the business of the organisation. Schools, universities and training courses cannot afford a high failure rate. They have a right to some way of determining who is likely to pass/succeed.

FOR REFLECTION

- Think about who has the responsibility of selection in groups you know.
- To what extent do members self-select in which groups? Why?

Texts about running therapeutic groups stress the importance of a pre-group assessment for suitability. I think that all texts I have read emphasise that group members should be carefully selected. But whose business is this selection? Is it not the potential participant who has the right and responsibility to decide whether this group will fulfil that participant's needs? In a radical departure from the usual practice, various colleagues and I have run therapeutic groups where **participants are free to self-select**.

On what basis would we exclude people? Because they are too unstable? One colleague ran an open therapeutic group on an acute adult inpatient unit (see Chapter 6). Lisa (Group 2) turned out to have a horrific background of trauma and would certainly not have been included in the ED group if there had been pre-group assessments, yet her psychometric scores post-group showed that she had made the most gains of any group member! Should we exclude those we deem to have antisocial personalities and to be untrustworthy? A good group can make sensible judgements along with some useful confrontation of avoided problems. Should we exclude those with avoidant attachment? They will probably exclude themselves but if they come can make important gains. With anxious attachment? They can make huge gains in a carefully run therapy group. Should we exclude those who talk too much? This would be nice for the facilitator but actually it's the facilitator's job to deal with unbalanced input from participants.

Maybe there is more risk if we allow members to self-select. Certainly managing 'problem personalities' presupposes a skilled facilitator in a true group where dynamics matter. If a number of people happen to share geographical or virtual space but don't need to interact with each other, management is much simpler. In this case there is simply an individual, educational and task focus (see Chapter 1). Some theorists would call this an **aggregate** (Burtis & Turman 2006) rather than a true group; a set of individuals sharing the same space but relating only to the material and minimally to each other, like an audience listening to a lecture. Burtis and Turman identify **interdependence** as being an essential characteristic of a group, contrasting this with independence (as in an aggregate) and dependence.

This 'easier to manage' effect of aggregates can be usefully applied to the management of 'true' groups of interdependent members. For the facilitator who is anxious about the potential interplay of personalities within a group, it is **best to have a clear structure**. Activities with their purpose and timings should be meticulously planned before the group starts.

3. PLANNING A SESSION

This planning should include not only what activities are going to happen in the session but who will be involved in each. They should take into account what time is available and the desired shape of the session (see next section). Here is an example of the planning for the first of eight sessions for a closed therapeutic group for Depression. There will be 10–12 participants and the group will take place from 6 to 9 pm.

What can be used to relax them as they arrive? It is probable (always) that some will arrive late. Should they have material (e.g. hand-outs) to read or should they just be left to chat? These ideas are unlikely to be helpful, as they are not energising. Since no one is likely to know anyone else, name tags will be written out for all as they arrive, with the name they want to be called. For the same reason, it seems useful to have an ice-breaker. Should this be a fun exercise (like finding someone whose favourite animal is the same as yours and discussing why this is the favourite) or more related to the perceived task?

We decide to have tea/coffee and biscuits available as people arrive and to start them working in pairs/triads as soon as about four participants are there, around the orienting task; 'Discuss what you would like to get out of this series of meetings'. This sentence is written up on a flip chart and the task can be continued until 15 minutes after the start time to allow everyone to join the process before formal introduction and so on. This has the effect of beginning to involve people with each other in very small groups, which will make them feel more relaxed with the larger group.

It seems to me important not to set pointless tasks. For this reason, the animal exercise and similar ice breakers were discarded, and the next activity should be collecting the ideas people have been discussing onto the flip chart as a guide for the coming sessions. It will form a check on what is wanted and on the expectations of participants. This should take until 6.30.

*Now we can do the short, formal introduction to the group and facilitators. Housekeeping rules. A **few** explicit ground rules, preferably generated also by the group. 6.45.*

Should we now focus on some educational input on depression? We certainly need to do so before the end of this meeting because it is essential that participants go away feeling that they have gained some knowledge and that the group will, hopefully, be useful to them in combating their depression. However, keeping the group interactive seems more important at this time. They are still strangers. They need to get to know each other at a level which is not superficial in order to profit from interdependence.

*We decide to move to an introductory exercise which is a favourite of mine because it cuts through too much reliance on talking and accesses deeply held values which resonate well across the group. This is the 'draw your **personal coat of arms**' exercise.*

Each participant is given a large sheet of paper and asked to draw a 'coat of arms' which has two to four images on it which express 'who you are as a person – what is really important to you'. It is emphasised that this is not an 'art' project – it doesn't matter how bad the drawing is.

When the drawings are done, each participant holds up the coat of arms and explains why those particular images have been chosen. Facilitators can model by also doing the exercise and presenting their coats of arms first. This has the added advantage of modelling how long the description should be. In any interaction (particularly in introductions) **group members will derive an implicit rule of 'how and how long I should speak' by following whoever goes first.** *By going first, the facilitator sets the style, subject range and length.*

When the drawings are done the facilitator can ask for comments and resonances. This will begin to pull the group together, as people explore the similarities and diversities of their identities and values.

This will take until about 7.30, which is a good time for a short tea and comfort break, as the resonances from the exercise will loosen people up to talk to each other informally. By 8.00 we come back together for a short lecture by a facilitator on depression with its symptoms and treatment ideas, not forgetting to begin externalising it (see Chapter 3) and to allow for questions and comments from participants. At 8.20 to 8.25 we divide people into groups of three or four. ('Pick someone you haven't talked to before') and ask them to discuss how depression impacts on their own lives. This exercise can be ended at 8.45 to 8.50. Back to whole group and people can be asked to share/comment on whatever they wish to from their previous discussion. This draws the group together into a whole for closing, with reminders of future times, contact details and so on.

The session planned above should feel relaxed and seamless to the participants but note that this is only so because the facilitators have put considerable thought into what happens when. When they are actually doing that session they must also watch the process and be prepared to build in flexibility – for example, monitoring the energy of conversations and adjusting time by cutting them shorter if they seem to be flagging. This is unusual. Usually time spent in small group discussions seems very short to participants, although it can seem very long to facilitators. My own general practice is for the facilitator/s not to join these small group discussions unless a group invites the facilitator in; for example, by asking a question.

4. WHO WILL WORK WITH WHOM?
Who works with whom can be complicated. If the group are all well known to each other they can be allowed to chat informally to their own friends when they arrive. However, this mix must be changed to cut through cliques and schisms. Small groups could be chosen, for example, by going round consecutively and giving numbers – 'One, two, three, four, one, two, three, four', and then asking those with the same numbers to form a group. This looks random but in fact breaks up those who are sitting together.

Sometimes, in working with a team, the facilitator might wish the small groups to reflect a mix of different professions. Part of the preparation for working with an extant group like a team is finding out the **dragons in the undergrowth**. The facilitator must try to learn before convening the group who gets along well or badly with whom and what issues are likely to come up to cause division or even to cause cohesion on the basis of out-group tensions. As we discussed in Chapter 1, out-group hostility and scapegoating feels comfortable and might need to run a little. However, it then needs to be reined in, as it is unlikely to be healthy in the wider system. Within-group hostilities must be explicitly addressed by facilitators, probably covertly. One way of doing this is to put people who dislike and usually avoid each other together in small group work in a task which is likely to increase their agreement and empathy with one another.

In some work groups, small group work may be based on interest in a particular sub-task. If people are particularly interested in or passionate about something, they will work harder in that area. Here the task itself determines the composition of the small group.

Whichever principles of deciding who works with whom in small groups, the issue should not be left to chance but should be a conscious and deliberate facilitative choice.

FOR REFLECTION

- Are there cliques in any of the groups you belong to?
- Would it be useful, or not, to break up these cliques? (Sometimes they may usefully be left as such, especially in very short-term groups where deeper group relationships are not necessary).
- How would you arrange subgroups for specific tasks in order to get the optimal pattern of interactions for that group?

The emotional shape of a session

A session is the time a group meets on one occasion. Facilitators must have a pattern in mind timed over the whole length of the session and **tight timekeeping (with some flexibility) is essential. This is absolutely the responsibility of the facilitator.**

Martha is a chief executive and is generally unpopular with the staff; she is seen as dictatorial and unduly focused on financial values rather than the stated mission values of the organisation. It is decided to have an away day for senior management to consider forward direction. A team of external consultants is tasked with facilitating the event.

The morning is filled with lecture-type input on the business plan and current financial constraints. The lack of interactive space makes most participants feel bored and resentful, seeing this day as 'the mixture as before'. The resentment is further fuelled in private conversations over the lunch break.

In the afternoon session, which is due to close at 3.30 pm, the facilitators introduce the issue of management style and open up interactive interchanges. There is a slow, hesitant start but critical voices begin to be heard and the conversation gains momentum as a full-scaled pillory of Martha. At 3.30 the day is closed with no summing up and no resolution for any of the problems expressed.

None of the participants feels that the day was useful. Martha has to take some sick leave for stress and comes back to work more defensive and dictatorial than ever. Some other participants feel that at least they 'told it like it is' but their bitterness about management style is greater even than before, making work even more stressful. Others find themselves embarrassed to have been part of the vicious lynch mentality which was unleashed. There is still more awkwardness than before in any interactions with Martha.

In this away day the facilitators have been guilty of very bad timing in terms of the emotional shape of the session. If we diagram emotional intensity for the day it might look something like this:

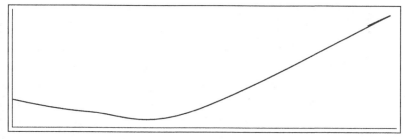

Figure 4.1 Emotional intensity of Martha's session

In other words, emotions were more and more aroused and especially escalated near the end of the day. At that point the facilitators ended; there was no closure. One might decide to do this deliberately but this would be unusual. Generally, the session shape should be as follows:

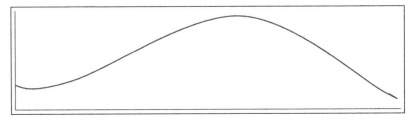

Figure 4.2 Emotional intensity of a usual session

When there is bad news to be given or a conflict to be dealt with, it makes sense to do so as near as possible to the beginning of the session, leaving plenty of time to mop up.

Keith is a new and fairly unpopular team leader, brought in by the organisation to make cuts in costs. He has some particularly bad news to give the team and a consultant is brought in to facilitate an away day. The consultant does the preparation necessary; finding out what the interpersonal relationships are like in the team, who works well and badly with whom and what message the organisation management wishes to convey.

After introductory exercises designed to access participants' core values there is a brief presentation on the team's tradition and history and then the floor is opened to Keith to present the givens and restraints within which the service will now have to be delivered. This creates a huge surge of anxiety and anger, little relieved by a question and answer session. In the lunch break it is noticeable that the atmosphere is tense and people avoid any talk about work and the work context.

Immediately after lunch the team is split into carefully designed small groups of three to five people, including in the groups those who rarely work with each other, with Keith allocated to one of them. They are tasked with finding creative solutions to some of the problems thrown up in the morning. These are briefly presented to the plenary and the day is pulled together with a celebration of the team core values.

This away day improves relationships in the team and members become much more inclined to appreciate Keith's difficulties and constraints. They proceed with a rise in morale in spite of the difficult climate; a sense of pride in what they are capable of doing as a team.

In this session the shape of emotional intensity was as follows:

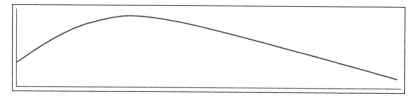

Figure 4.3 Emotional intensity of Keith's session

Which emotions?

So, we need to attend to emotional intensity. A further question for facilitators: which emotion? Some emotions drive us apart, others bring us together.

Anxiety is important. Some social anxiety is always present in a group; we all need to determine how socially safe we are. Different people have different responses to this anxiety, depending on which strategies they developed as children. Note attachment theory in this regard. If we feel at all under attack we all defend ourselves (become defensive) but we have very different ways of doing this.

Some of us retreat, hide, feel an increase of insecurity and a decrease of confidence. We avoid interacting, as in avoidant attachment style. This distances us from others as they find it more difficult to 'read' us and therefore become less confident themselves. They experience us as cold and possibly as rejecting of them. I have been fascinated at the way very shy people are often seen as 'stuck-up' when in fact their internal experience is the opposite. They tend to be seeing themselves as worse than others, not better.

Some of us become hostile and aggressive. This reaction is even more distancing. Anger, hostility, aggression are the most threatening of all emotions. The increase in threat amplifies the defensive responses of the other. An escalation of aggression, anxiety, defensiveness ensues. This causes some to become equally angry and aggressive, others to become over-active peacemakers, willing to sacrifice task, ideas and congruence in a desperate attempt to placate the aggressor. It is important to remember that this **dysfunctional placating is driven by fear and is not the same as the facilitator task of reducing and resolving conflict.** Facilitators should be determined to deal with anger and conflict but they should not be afraid of it, or avoiding and placating might replace resolving.

So, **Avoidance**, **Anger** and **Aggression** push people Away.

Sadness and vulnerability, on the other hand, **draw people closer** as they tend to arouse empathy.

Emma was taking part in a training exercise in which she had to interview someone while two others took the roles of observers. She experienced the observation comments as very critical of her and felt hurt and defensive. Fortunately, instead of attacking or blaming, she was enabled to screw up her courage and explain how she was feeling and why. This allowed more explanation of how the observers were thinking, along with apologies from them about having inadvertently undermined her. Her courage in being willing to expose her vulnerability made the group closer and better informed about each other's thoughts.

Although in contrast to sadness and vulnerability, **happiness and laughter** also **draw people together**. Humour can be very important, though not humour which is veiled aggression. Expressions of compassion and empathy are particularly important in strengthening relationships. Above all, it is important for emotions to be congruent. **People are distanced from each other if they sense any insincerity.**

The developmental stage of a group

Just as a session has a shape in terms of its emotional intensity, so a group has a developmental lifespan. It is essential for a facilitator to recognise this and to shape the group accordingly.

When we are exposed to a roomful of strangers we all experience social anxiety. This is functional. We are going to need to assess many things; how we fit, how safe they are in the areas in which we feel vulnerable, what roles we should adopt, whether they will value our contributions. A lot of our mental energy at first, whether we realise this or not, is going into observing those around us. We decide who we like and who we don't, who makes us feel safe and who threatens us. We automatically assess who is powerful and who is popular. This is an absolutely critical time in the development of a group, when the culture should be set. We discuss this setting of the culture in this section.

As people get to know each other the group settles in terms of its overall degree of cohesion and comfort. The interactive network and mode of being in that context have solidified into some habitual patterns. The culture develops inertia and becomes difficult to change. People have chosen who they are closest to. If the culture has been set well in the early stages this is a good time for deepening engagement. It is also a time when group tasks should be able to be performed with a minimum loss of efficiency.

Some groups have a definite end. If this is so, there is an ending stage as well, when the tasks are to consolidate gains made in the group, prepare for post-group gains and deal with the inevitable loss of relationships.

Starting a group: setting the culture

In the example above of planning a first session we can see that the facilitator/s must be well prepared to set the culture. There has been much written about group contracting; for example, in the field of group supervision. A contract defines the purpose for meeting, the logistics (when, where, how often, how many times, for how long at a time) and the rules of interaction. Some of these rules are explicit 'ground rules'. The contract is negotiated and often written in the first session. It can, of course, be modified later, but it is generally seen that the inception of the group is the time for contracting.

A written contract is very useful in making very clear the things which have been explicit and agreed. The setting of ground rules and house-keeping, including limits of confidentiality, can be foundational later for positive group process. In this explicit contract we consider such issues as what relationships or contacts members may form outside group time. It is important for the facilitator to acknowledge that processes outside the group sessions are never really controllable. For example, although most groups like confidentiality rules as part of their contract, absolute confidentiality can never be guaranteed and members need to remember this when they communicate personal material. Similarly, it is up to members themselves whether they make contact outside the group time. It is generally better to assume that this might happen and contract for how it might happen. Do they want to exchange email addresses or phone numbers? Here is a chance for them to opt out if they do not wish to do so.

However, the implicit rules of a group are almost more important. These are the implicit (process) rules relating to power dynamics and other issues. They are even more important than the explicit contract and need to be put in place as early as possible. They constitute the group culture. Of course the culture changes as time goes on but, as for the explicit rules, the first session is a critical time. It is at this time that the culture of the group is set. Like the contract, it could be modified later but this would be more difficult.

So, how do we set the culture? What do we need in terms of culture for any group to work well together? We have discussed this at length in previous chapters but let us summarise here. For any group of any kind to be considered a successful group the task/s should be enhanced by the relational factor. In other words, what is to be achieved should be achieved better if there is more than one person involved. Because we are relational beings, this will be true of many if not most tasks but only under the following conditions.

1. Members should be **interdependent** (Burtis & Turman 2006). When group members are not working in collaboration with each other they might as well be individuals. When they are too dependent **group think** becomes a problem (Brown 2000) and some of the contribution which members might make becomes suppressed by the culture of the group itself.
2. Members must trust each other.
3. The culture must be characterised by respect for all opinions offered, with robust mechanisms for reaching consensus where this is essential or for holding contradictory ideas in an accepting atmosphere.
4. Members should have a positive view of the status/importance/usefulness of the group itself and of themselves within the group.

The attitudes which participants are to have towards each other need to be modelled and set by the facilitator from the start. **Radical listening** is really important. When members see the facilitator welcoming **every** contribution as important and being really respectful and curious about what that person is trying to communicate, they learn to do the same. It is important at this stage not to be at all critical or rejecting. Very anxious members will be watching carefully to decide whether it is safe for them to make any contribution. Any response which looks like a put down or dismissal, even to what someone else has said, will be experienced as threatening and silence that participant for the future.

If a difference of opinion arises, that is a particular opportunity, so the facilitator should be alert and pick up on it immediately. Stop the conversation and say something like;

Just a minute, this is really interesting. You (turning to A) think ... (summarise A's position) and you (turning to B) think ... (summarise B's position). That's great! – it gives us a binocular view. Let's explore more about why you each think the way you do ...

The importance of using this technique for disagreement or difference of viewpoint cannot be emphasised enough. It gives the message that **even contradictory viewpoints are acceptable and that no judgement needs to be made between them** (more on this in Chapter 5 when we address how to deal with dyadic conflict). The exploration of why each protagonist thinks in a particular way uncovers values and begins the development of the assumption of good faith on the part of all participants. It cuts through the potential for conflict. Remember how we made the point in Chapter 1 that conflict is not healthy and should always be resolved as quickly as possible but that, on the other hand, disagreement is part of a creative process which makes more thinking and information available.

When this message is given early in the life of the group, members become accepting of difference and of the thought processes and values of the others. In fact they can celebrate difference and variety of ideas. They become able to disagree with each other without getting hostile and defensive. The facilitator begins to draw together a concordance of values, especially if it is possible to dig down to the common values which underlie differences of thinking.

Stacey has joined a supervision group at work and feels nervous because she is new in the job and her manager, Joe, is also in the group. On one matter which comes up, however, she disagrees so strongly with him that she gets angry and finds the courage to say he is wrong. Glenda, the supervisor, seems interested in why their opinions are so different and asks more about what she and Joe are thinking. Stacey stops being angry because she is being respectfully heard. In the discussion she realises that she and Joe are both motivated by the same values, even though they think very differently about how these can best be served. At the end of the discussion they still disagree but she understands how he is thinking and believes that he, in his turn, understands and respects her viewpoint.

Bouncing the ball: nuances of engagement

One way to ensure that all knowledges are available is a technique I call **'bouncing the ball around the room'**. If one person talks too much and the facilitator keeps an individual focus, other individuals in the group can disengage and there is a loss of relationship and focus. Bouncing the ball around the room means picking up from what the participant is saying and asking for comment from another member of the group.

This can be done randomly but more may sometimes be achieved by using a rule to decide whose comment should be sought. The rule will depend on what the facilitator is trying to achieve in the moment and will be based on observation of non-verbal communication (see Chapter 2).

1. It may be that someone really feels *very* uncomfortable being asked to comment. Since the facilitator is trying not to escalate anxiety, this is *not* the person to ask.
2. Someone might already be 'glazing over'. If this person is asked to comment it forces re-engagement with the process – but remember that it might also put the person 'on the spot' and can increase anxiety or even hostility. At any rate there should be an implicit rule that commenting can be declined. Move on quickly if anyone is clearly stuck for an answer or embarrassed about being asked to comment. Nevertheless, this ball-bouncing tendency in the facilitator will discourage disengagement.
3. This is a good way to bring in the 'alternative knowledge' of a relatively silent participant. It is important to remember that if a comparatively diffident, unconfident member comments, the rule of welcoming *all* contributions with enthusiasm and respectful consideration of the ideas expressed is particularly important. At a whiff of criticism or disregard of ideas this person might become even more silent.
4. A particular kind of alternative knowledge which can be accessed in this way is that of a child in a group which includes adults. A child below puberty will usually be more comfortable with a physical task (like drawing) rather than sitting formally talking. This child is probably still listening attentively, however, and can be invited to express an opinion by 'bouncing the ball'.
5. Someone might have signalled an emotional reaction by a movement or change of expression. Going straight to this person can intensify the process and deepen engagement, as long as the reaction is handled with empathy.
6. The whole room might be asked to comment on 'what resonates' or 'what this thought brings to mind'. This can only be done in a group where there is already enough trust for people to be willing to volunteer comments. It also has the possible disadvantage of letting the dominant voices take up more space, so a deliberate bouncing the ball to the more silent members may still be necessary.

As explained in the account of radical listening, the most important thing about making people realise that their comments and ideas are valued is to **use** those ideas and *refer* to them, acknowledging **whose** they are. After bouncing the ball, or indeed in any conversation, it is useful for the facilitator to refer to what has been said and who said it, weaving these suggestions into any summary of what is needed.

As you suggested, Brian, we could ... Remember that Doreen made the point that ... We shouldn't forget what Ahmed pointed out, that ...

Silences and mindfulness

As explained in Chapter 3, short silences, thoughtful silences, are very important in a Systemic Narrative approach. If we want creativity, reflectiveness or an accessing of less known knowledge, there must be enough reflective space to access this. A good group facilitator will allow or even promote such silences. They might be prompted by an open question or by a very resonating statement made by a group member. Sometimes they may be part of a **Mindfulness** (Williams & Penman 2011) exercise.

Mindfulness is a meditative practice sometimes used to help with anxiety or depression, in the same way as deep relaxation used to be popular. It has the advantage over deep body relaxation in being quicker and easier to induce or self-induce. Participants usually close their eyes and start with noticing sensory input. They might be directed to notice their breath, what they hear, what they feel, the pressure of their legs on the chair, and so on. They 'watch' their thoughts without trying to control or modify them and without attaching the usual emotional reactions or value judgements. This is a way of training the person practising mindfulness in being less anxious about thoughts and gaining a more objective stance towards them. It is a practice achieving something of the same results as externalising but also using the effects of a relaxed, trance-like state.

Mindfulness can be used with groups and has been dealt with extensively in a large body of literature (see, for example, Williams & Penman 2011) as it is currently very popular. We will not discuss specifics of mindfulness techniques. We mention it now because there is a similarity between this and a relaxed reflective and silent space which may be used for generating creativity or problem solving and particularly for recalling memories which belong to the alternative knowledge.

We must remember, however, that silence can be very anxiety-provoking. Generally in social situations we do not tolerate periods of silence except with people we feel very close to. In Chapter 1 we referred to some group work where anxiety is deliberately engendered by a refusal of the facilitator to structure the discourse or break any silences. In our way of facilitating this will happen rarely if at all. Keeping silent in order to facilitate the finding of lost information to thicken the story (Chapter 3) is different, though even this might sometimes engender some anxiety. The facilitator will minimise that by giving encouragement prompts.

The 'what are you all thinking?' round

A technique for increasing the variety of available ideas which also slightly deepens relationships is the 'what are you all thinking?' round. This should probably not be done until the group has reached a later stage of development with some trust and ease already in place.

I usually bring this in when the group has fallen into a natural silence. After letting it run for a short while, ask everyone to hold onto what they are thinking about at that precise moment. Then go round the group asking all to report what this is. It is very important (as always) to be accepting of whatever comes up. Some people may be thinking of their summer holidays or other matters irrelevant to the discussion. This doesn't matter. The important thing is that it gives a snapshot at a particular moment in time of the **individual internal interactions within the group dialogue**.

In this exercise, like the introductory exercise of 'draw your personal coat of arms', I discourage comments or resonances on the first round of reporting. Even without conversation, participants are very influenced in their reporting by what the others have already said; however, in this exercise there is usually a great natural variety of responses as members will have been cognitively led in an infinite number of different directions. After all have reported what they were thinking when the action stopped, the facilitator can ask for resonances and thoughts on what the others have expressed (again as is done in the personal coat of arms exercise). This invitation to reflect and resonate increases diversity of thinking and depth of knowledge and relating.

May I emphasise that this kind of exercise is not only for therapy groups. It works equally well with work or educational groups and increases creativity and available knowledge around a task.

In all conversations, group members speak for themselves. If we want to know what someone is thinking we ask them; we do not hypothesise or make assumptions. As we explained when we introduced radical listening, we need to be always curious about what the other is trying to express, as far as possible not allowing our own constructions to get in the way. We must always make the assumption of good faith and strongly question or even counter our negative constructions – 'He is just selfish', 'she has a personality disorder', 'he is arrogant', 'she is stupid'. This direct and valuing style of communication starts with the facilitator, whose modelling can engender it in the whole group without explicit critiquing of less functional styles.

So, it is important for members to communicate as clearly and directly as possible, owning their own opinions and emotional reactions. Unfortunately, this can be difficult because of the necessity of defending self, so that some people are silenced, some prefer indirect or ambiguous communication and some will be influenced to express only the 'party line', that is, the dominant opinion, or that which they see as belonging with the power in the group. Some communication is diverted and some is repressed. Early and consistent radical listening by the facilitator, alongside techniques like small group work, which help the members to grow closer together, will break down defensiveness over time and communication styles should become more assertive and direct.

FOR REFLECTION

- How confident do you feel to express clearly what you think, whatever the group pressure to conform to another opinion?
- How inclined might you be to complain to someone else rather than speak directly to someone with whom you have an issue or disagreement?
- If you feel too afraid to express yourself directly to the relevant person/s, what can make you feel more confident?
- Do you think that sometimes other people might be afraid to speak directly to you?
- What might help them be more confident in being able to disagree with you?

Starting with a group which has been ongoing before the facilitator joins

Because it is harder to change an already set culture there are particular challenges for the facilitator coming into a group which has been ongoing. When all members of a group are new to each other there is comparatively a tabula rasa. All are anxious; all are feeling their way. Proactive facilitation work, as suggested above, can start the culture off in a healthy way so that the group can maximise its potential to grow and be optimally functional. However, when the facilitator joins later, there are already networks of likes and dislikes. The group culture might not be healthy at all. People might not trust each other; there might be defensiveness and hidden (or even open) hostilities. They might have an expectation that the facilitator (especially if the role is that of manager or team leader) will be looking for ways to criticise or undermine them. For new groups, a healthy culture can often be set in the first session; for an already established group this might take quite some time.

Ideally, a facilitator entering such a group should have some prior knowledge of what the potential problems are, the **dragons in the undergrowth**, as suggested above; prior information from as many of the group members as possible about how they see the group, who gets along how with who, what morale is like. What does the group as a whole want from the new facilitator or leader?

Jennifer was the new manager for a team of four IT developers. She knew that Jason, who was still in the team, had applied for her position and therefore resented the fact that she had been appointed. She had also learned before taking up her role that Joan and Terry did not get along. They were said to have a 'personality clash'. Bill was a loner who preferred just interacting with his computer, not with people.

The problem set by Jason proved the easiest to solve. Jennifer had a one-to-one with him soon after she started in which she deliberately opened up the issue of her appointment and how he might/must feel about it. She apologised and assured him that she respected his skill set. In the team interactions she deferred to his consultative opinion often, though not always, since she was also making sure that the ideas of the others could be expressed and used. This particularly applied to Bill, whose thoughts had to be specifically drawn out. Generally, she went with Bill's personal preference, however, and gave him the projects which were better executed individually rather than with teamwork.

*She had to work hardest on the Joan and Terry dyad, using the **dyadic conflict model** (Chapter 5) and encouraging them to work together, often with her presence, to draw out their mutual values and personal pressures. They grew more and more able over time to work collegiately, though they never became close friends.*

Sometimes the dragons in the undergrowth may be too powerful, even for a skilled facilitator, as in the next vignette. In this case, as Simon does, we just have to go for the best possible fit.

Simon was the new supervisor for a team of six therapists. The team had gone through some important recent changes. The previous team leader, who was still involved in clinical work in the team, had been promoted to a higher management position. Two other members of the team competed for her position and the more senior was resentful because the other was given the promotion.

In the first supervision session these three senior members of the team were absent for various reasons and the three more junior members expressed a need to use supervision sessions principally for looking at team dynamics, presumably because these had been so difficult for them. The contract had to be re-negotiated in the second session when the senior members of the team were present. They seemed firmly opposed to spending time looking at team dynamics and wanted to focus on clinical material only. The juniors were unwilling or unable to express their own preferences at this time.

As the months went on Simon tried to weave in something of both of these demands and introduced some exercises, like the 'draw your coat of arms' one, intended to bring people together. However, the team remained split in this way until the senior members at various times had left. Good clinical supervision could take place but the junior members remained unwilling to express anything about the team which might run counter to what the more senior participants thought, unless those more senior people were absent. Simon had no wider system leverage in the organisation and was unable to meet separately with the seniors. Only after they left did it become possible to negotiate a change of contract, which included much more team self-reflection and personal closeness.

Both Jennifer and Simon in the above examples were influenced by the principle of utilisation (see Chapter 2). They used what was there and the natural personality trends and inclinations of group members – as well as trying to change dysfunctional patterns.

The open group: when new members join

In the above examples, a new facilitator (or leader) joined an already formed group with its own developed culture and history. Although most therapy or focus groups are closed, this does not apply to more naturally formed groups, which are open. This is not an absolute category. Open groups in which there is a majority of new members (see, for example, the account of the open acute ward group in Chapter 6) are more like new groups. In work teams and other supervision and therapy groups only one or two members join at any given time.

In this kind of open group, the new member has not yet become acculturated and is in a different group developmental phase from the other members. Attention must be paid to this new member to help make the joining process as quick and easy as possible. Most organisations offer new employees some kind of initiation designed to integrate them and acquaint them with important aspects of the organisation. More is ideally needed. A temporary mentoring or buddy system in the team can help. Special attention should be paid by the facilitator/leader, though this need not be too overt. Usually, the culture of the group is robust enough not to be substantially altered by the new member but there should be concerted efforts to bring this person into the culture. The facilitator will have to decide whether early group stage exercises and processes are appropriate or whether these would interrupt the group developmental stage and so will have to be truncated and made into a more individual process for the new person.

The group review

Reviewing should be an ongoing process in any group, in that potential times for discussing what is happening and what needs to happen should be built into all sessions. Nevertheless, it is useful to have a more definite and formal review planned. How frequent this should be depends on the group and its purpose and functions.

In a short-term group, the review naturally takes place at the end. However, although this gives information which might be useful for future groups, it is not useful in modifying the working of this one. I believe, therefore, that there should be a **mid-term review** as well, to check progress and give a chance to change what might need to be changed. This might not need to take a whole session but ideally time should not be skimped. As has been indicated throughout this book, the review must include evaluating the task progress but also the relationship/process factors. What questions need to be asked will depend on the specific group.

In a long-term or permanent group, a sensible time between reviews can be determined, again depending on the unique needs. Some teams have meetings every week. How often these need include the relationship/process factors must be decided in each situation. I would think that minimum would be about every six months.

The review should be 360 degrees. It should include evaluation of the facilitator as well as the task and participants and should be made as safe as possible. Anonymity of questionnaires is often employed but this might not be as safe as it seems if the team/group is relatively small, as it is often rather obvious who has answered how. More useful is to have an outsider collect and collate comments.

Some reviews may be done in a conversation, but here the nuisance variables of social pressure come into play. Can one afford to criticise the facilitator or other figure seen as powerful? Can one afford to disagree with the majority? Can one disagree with a best friend? Obviously, the healthier the culture the more these could happen, but it is not useful to assume that the culture is healthy because it seems so, especially if the facilitator's perceptions are driving the evaluation plans.

As a facilitator, I find reviews terrifying. This is where I invite potential criticism and make it as easy as possible for that to happen with no opportunity for repercussions. But if I am expecting and engendering openness, frankness and a lack of defensiveness in participants, I need to be open, frank and non-defensive myself. The extent to which I have a position which cannot be critiqued is the extent to which I might be fooling myself that I am doing a good job and that all is well. Real feedback is essential and I need to promote honest feedback loops wherever possible.

FOR REFLECTION

- How can you get honest feedback for your role in a particular group to which you belong?
- Think about a group you know and how you would build in evaluation.
- How would you handle negative feedback? What would help you?
- How could you yourself critique without being too threatening or backing away from issues?

Summary

In this chapter we considered how to plan and start a group, how to set the culture, group development over time and how to consider emotional intensity, both in a session and across the life of the group. We looked particularly at the importance of implicit rules, thinking about how the facilitator could model and engender positive ones, to keep the dynamics healthy. Very specific principles and techniques were described for achieving good process.

FOR REFLECTION

- Go back over the chapter and list the techniques and ideas you would find useful.
- Think about how they might be applied in some groups you know.

5

SPECIFIC PROCESS ISSUES

Good and bad conformity

We all have a tendency to conform to the opinions of the majority. There are many explanations in different domains as to why this should be so; anthropological theories, neurological theories, psychological theories. The why is not important in facilitating group dynamics, so we will not be considering these theories. What we do need to look at is what the effects of the phenomenon are on group functioning. When and how is conformity good and useful and when is it damaging, either to the task, the group or the individual?

This conformity is something which has always fascinated social psychologists and some of the most classic experiments in Social Psychology have examined various facets of the phenomenon. We have a tendency to try to reach consensus with those we relate to and will often sacrifice our own opinions to those of the majority, the powerful, or the higher status members of our group. Conformity makes sense if we are co-constructing reality but too much conformity will result in the 'thin story' (White 2007). We have emphasised in previous chapters the importance in a group of accessing all opinions and some ways of doing this. In summary:

1. Model radical listening from the beginning.
2. Accept all opinions respectfully as valid.
3. Greet the earliest possible sign of disagreement with enthusiasm as a binocular or multi-ocular view, exploring in detail the viewpoints expressed without any pressure for agreement.
4. Bounce the ball around the room, particularly involving the more silent or unconfident members.

As a group develops its culture, members themselves take on the style and techniques of the facilitator. Throughout this book we have supported the principle of giving away skills by modelling and even by directly informing. The origin of group culture is the leader or facilitator, although members also bring in their own individual styles and skills. The group is greater than its parts.

Groupthink is a term given to a group in which there seems to be no variation of opinion between members (Brown 2000). Consensus is generally useful and the successful completion of most tasks requires at least a rough consensus to be reached without too much hesitation. However, if there is only one dominant idea and the whole group seems to adhere to it with no dissention, the advantage of a group with its multiple knowledges is lost. Even an individual working alone will be more able to examine and critique the idea than a group characterised by groupthink.

Usually groupthink will arise because there is a very powerful individual or clique whose ideas cannot be challenged by anyone else. Brown (2000) quotes research showing that the most important variable in whether groupthink occurs is in the leadership. Fodor and Smith found that if the leader is 'power-hungry', less information and fewer alternatives are generated. Leader directiveness was investigated by Peterson, who distinguished between directiveness around goal (leaders driving forward their own opinion) and directiveness around process; for example, leaders ensuring that all participants were heard, or that decisions were made in good time. The first was linked with bad decision making, and the second with good decision making.

The phenomenon can also occur when the group has a very strong need for group cohesion and there is a strong implicit rule to maintain social harmony as the highest value. This can particularly happen when the wider environment is experienced by the group as threatening. On the other hand, it might also happen in an 'old' group where people have become very comfortable with their mutual thoughts and are beginning to settle into habits of doing things. They have developed a group subjective reality, which has become the thin story and reduces creativity.

> *If they all give the appearance of total agreement on some issue, then we may be led to the conclusion that this view is the only valid one. Such a state of mind is likely to inhibit any creative search for other opinions, and even to lead to a positive rejection of those opinions and a ridiculing of their sources.* (Brown 2000, p. 213)

Weingarten (1998) says:

> *I no longer regard the appearance of consensus among class members as a moment to move on, but rather as a moment to pause and ask people to reflect on whether or not the seeming agreement takes into account all of what they wish to discuss. The times when people notice that they are holding back some of their thoughts and feelings have been enormously instructive to all of us with regard to understanding how, even with the best of intentions, group processes can marginalize some experiences of some people some of the time.*

This pause to consider which knowledges are being lost in the consensus is therefore extremely useful in keeping open the creative potential of the group.

Throughout this chapter it will become apparent why certain practices expounded earlier in the book are so important. The outright rejection of an opinion and ridiculing of the source, whether in-group or out-group, should not happen if the culture of respect and radical listening has been developed. I hope that what we have already discussed about promoting and valuing disagreement, with exploration of the details and foundations of that disagreement, would militate against the development of groupthink. In the next section we will take up the issue of power and how that affects group thinking.

We also have to note the balance between making people more comfortable (and less anxious) and when new challenges should be introduced. The **evaluation of the comfort-challenge dynamic is an ongoing task of the facilitator.** For example, comfort needs to be optimised by the facilitator of a newly formed group where individual anxieties are likely to be high. Change and challenge needs to be introduced when the group is becoming too settled. The facilitator should be 'taking the comfort temperature' throughout the life of the group. We remember that performance is optimised in a medium state of arousal (anxiety) – the well-known inverted 'u' of the Yerkes-Dodson law of 1908. When the group has become very comfortable that is the opportune time to stretch it by introducing an exercise or subject that might have been too difficult when there was less comfort. If this does not happen, habit and boredom can set in.

The opposite problem from too much conformity is too little conformity. A group characterised by wrangling or by too much indulgence in discussion without conclusions is usually ineffectual. Positive process can be seriously undermined by power struggles within groups.

FOR REFLECTION

- Think of a group in which you feel very comfortable. Do you think group-think might have set in or is there plenty of space for diversity and disagreement?
- This book advocates facilitators and leaders being directive (controlling) about process but not about content. Think about leaders you know and consider where they fall on these dimensions.
- How might you break up too strong consensus if you were facilitating a group?

Power

One fruitful way to model what happens in groups of people is to think in terms of power, or personal power. What do we mean by this? The concept is difficult to define, though often easily recognised. Personal power is the ability to influence others, to move them in one direction or another. We might equate it with the ability to be noticed by others. This is not necessarily true; sometimes the most saliently noticeable person in a group is not the most influential.

- Overt power is characterised by being noticed and listened to, often by giving directions and orders, by an authoritative and sometimes authoritarian stance.
- Covert power is characterised by the ability to 'manipulate'; to influence others without their being aware of this influence.

Both of these descriptions contain words which can be seen as pejorative. Personal power generally has a bad press, except when we speak of someone as having 'charisma'. For this reason, some people like to pretend that they do not have power. There is another dynamic feeding into this. We are often more aware of ourselves as reactive than as proactive. 'I do what I do in response to what you did'. We punctuate circular causality in such a way that we see ourselves as controlled by the (proactive) input of others. Often we can't see our own power. Some people, in denying their power, have to use only covert methods of influence. This is where passive-aggressive manoeuvres come in – more about this later in the chapter. Actually, both overt and covert methods are important and both should be used appropriately. **Personal power is not the problem. It is the abuse of power, or too substantial**

variations of power, which cause problems. There will always be variations of power, although these are not by any means as obvious or static as usually conceptualised. In themselves they are not problematic but they may become so. It is essential that the facilitator continues to monitor them.

First, the facilitator always has personal power as a consequence of the facilitative function. This is inevitable, and denying it does not make for good facilitation; it must be managed responsibly. Actually, a group becomes angry with a facilitator who either doesn't have, or is unwilling to, exercise facilitative power. How many of us have ground our teeth in a meeting where the chair allows one person to dominate, or over-runs or gets through only half of the agenda because of poor timekeeping or process control.

My own bias, supported by much research on well-functioning groups and organisations (see, for example, Bunker & Alban 1997, Kottler & Englar-Carlson 2010) is that the power hierarchy in a group should be flattened as far as possible. This involves the facilitator in giving away power, especially to the less powerful.

So, how do we give away power? One way is to invite reviews of our own process and, most importantly, to accept those views with non-defensive curiosity. This can be quite difficult to do but is a skill which facilitators should learn.

Fred Facilitator: *I am aware that I got quite passionate about that just then and some of you looked a bit taken aback. (Turns to a generally less confident and silent member.) Barbs, how did it affect you?*

Barbs: *It was okay ...*

Fred: *It's kind of you to say that but I'm not sure that it was. You looked quite anxious.*

Barbs: *Well, I do get a bit nervous when people raise their voices, but I'm sure that's my fault ...*

Fred: *Well. In this instance it might be MY fault! (Taking the pressure off Barbs, to another group member) I guess you noticed my raised voice too – what do you think it might have said to the group?*

Bill: *Well, I think it told us quite clearly that we had better not disagree with you!*

Fred: *Oh dear, I really must apologise to all of you. I do get carried away sometimes and I really don't want to block your opinions. Can we go back to that and ask for someone who disagreed with me to say why. Then we might be able to see some way my thinking should be changed. At the very least we should get the richness of some alternative ideas ...*

Commenting on process and dropping hypotheses on the floor

In the above vignette the facilitator comments on the process in so far as it relates to his own behaviour in order to invite a review and flatten the power hierarchy. Commenting on the process can also perform other functions. For example, if the above had been a therapy group he might have wanted to pick up on Barbs' customary anxious response to help her wonder why she was so afraid of raised voices and what she could do to prevent this habit of interaction from silencing her own voice. It is often useful to invite disagreement and reality thickening in the group by watching to see who is giving a non-verbal message of dissent and bouncing the ball to that person. Alternatively, support can be elicited from the group. In the above example Fred deliberately invokes a more confident member to support Barbs' reaction. Of course, especially as a group develops, these comments on process and support are not supplied only by the facilitator. Increasingly the members themselves provide facilitative functions.

Dropping a hypothesis on the floor is a narrative alternative to interpretation, deliberately structured to lessen the facilitator's power and invite alternative knowledges. This involves the facilitator in making a guess, maybe about what someone is (or people are) thinking, what motivates them, what they would like. But the facilitator is not the expert on this knowledge, so the guess must be made very tentatively and followed by a pause for reactions. This silence is essential. The technique is designed to move things on and open conversational space. Its effect should not be to increase, but rather to decrease, the power and centrality of the facilitator and invite in disparate voices. Whether they agree or disagree is not important. The practice thickens and increases the knowledge available to the group and especially moves into what has never yet been said.

FOR REFLECTION

- Have you tried commenting on the process in a group or conversation? What happened?
- If you make a guess about someone else's thinking do you make space for them to edit, or might they feel they can't disagree with you?

Healthy communication

Some really bad communication habits are fairly endemic among human beings and they relate to felt personal power, or in fact its lack. We are extraordinarily **fearful of possible rejection by other people**. When they have offended us or we have offended them or have some other problems arising out of our interaction with them, they are the last ones we want to talk to about the issue. Instead of sorting out the problem with them we indulge in a variety of dysfunctional manoeuvres.

1. We avoid speaking about it at all. This might seem useful but 'bottling things up' can make us angrier over time and resolves nothing. The only time when it's alright not to speak about a problem is when it is so small that we can dismiss it and not think about it again.
2. We speak about it when we are angry. Anger is an energiser and makes us override our rejection concerns. Unfortunately, it also makes us stop listening or reasoning. **If we talk about a problem when we are angry we are likely to escalate it**.
3. We speak to other people about it. This feels comfortable but actually amounts to malicious gossip and plays havoc with our networks of relationships.

Jesus gave some very explicit directions on how to sort out problems with another. Over time I have applied them both personally and clinically, and find that when I do apply them, communication works much better than when I fail to do so. They are as follows:

1. It is the responsibility of whoever is aware of the problem, whether the offender or offended, to find a time to discuss the issue calmly with the other.
2. The discussion should be one-to-one in the first instance and happen when the two are calm. It should be characterised by radical listening and clarity of expressing one's own point of view. Of course, we cannot require that the other acts like this, but we can take care to do so ourselves.
3. If this does not reach a satisfactory conclusion, we should get one or two 'facilitators' to join our next discussion on the issue.
4. If this also fails, we can take the discussion to the wider group for resolution.

5. We should apologise if necessary and graciously accept apology in a forgiving spirit.
6. Communication should be congruent; lying is not functional.

In our group, we would want all communication to be as healthy as possible. We have already seen (Chapter 2) that anxiously or avoidantly attached individuals are very unlikely to be able to engage in the direct and non-defensive kind of communication we have here described. It is necessary within the group to provide the secure base which makes healthy communication possible. Even those who are securely attached will avoid communicating directly in situations they perceive as threatening. This avoidance leads to the silences and indirect communications detailed above, which in turn escalate conflict, whether overt or covert.

FOR REFLECTION

- In your own religion, personal philosophy or culture, what ideas are there about what constitutes good communication?
- Do they agree with those which I have stated above?
- Evaluate your own communication patterns. Do you want to modify them?
- What would help you to do so?

Covert conflict (the silent dissenters) cannot be directly managed in itself. It is necessary to apply all the principles of creating group health in order for the silenced to be able to have their voices, even when making statements which might threaten to lead them into conflict or cause rejection by the group or facilitator. Non-defensiveness, radical listening, compassionate acceptance must all be modelled.

We now consider what the facilitator should do to manage overt conflict, whether between facilitator and group or between different group members.

Conflict with, or attack directed at, the facilitator

It is immensely important for the facilitator to model and encourage non-defensiveness. If attacked, it is vital **not to attack back, even in a covert fashion**. It is important to note here that humour can mask a passive-aggressive response, even to oneself. Instead the attack should either be deflected by a natural move to another subject or by a non-defensive exploration of why it is happening. The latter is probably best left until later, when the attacker might be less angry and when the facilitator can be very sure to have the right attitude. If the issue might be very sensitive for the member, it might be better to have this discussion in a dyad rather than in the group, at least in the first instance.

As far as possible **no one in the group should feel attacked by the group leader**. If the facilitator does say something which is attacking, or is experienced as attacking, prompt and sincere apology is a good model for members to see. If it happens inadvertently, say because the member was frequently criticised in childhood and has developed a process habit of believing that others must be being critical, the apology is still necessary, rather than justification. In this case it is important for the facilitator to seek even more opportunities to support and encourage the member, possibly with some gentle later reference to and tackling of the process habit which needs deconstructing. The whole group culture should be containing if the principles in the previous chapter have been followed. Therefore, the group process should be healing and deconstructive in itself.

One way to cut through conflict if the facilitator is involved is to use the model of **symmetrical** and **complementary escalation** (Watzlawick et al. 2011). An understanding of these patterns in human interaction is useful if we find we are caught up as protagonists in any conflict or potential conflict. We diagram this below.

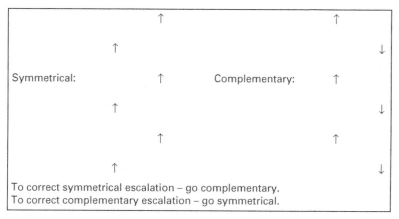

Figure 5.1 Symmetrical and complementary escalation

Symmetrical escalation is the classic model of wars and fights. One side goes 'one up' and the other applies more power and tops the first side, which then applies more aggression or force, which is then countered by even more aggression or force and so on. One side sends one rocket; the other sends three and causes more devastation than the one. The first side then sends five. The second sends ten. And so on ...

Complementary escalation is an opposite pattern. Here one side aggresses or produces a particular class of behaviour. The other side, in response, retreats or produces an opposite behaviour. This can happen, for example, when a relatively talkative person interacts with a relatively silent one. The talker is met with silence so talks more. This makes the silent person even more silent. Which makes the talker talk more. And so on.

The solution for both kinds of escalation is to go to the opposite. To cut through symmetrical escalation, go complementary. To cut through complementary escalation, go symmetrical. If the talker stops talking the silent one will say something. If the silent one starts talking the talker will say less. If a disagreement is escalating into conflict, 'You are right. I'm sorry,' usually stops it in its tracks. Or, if it would be dishonest in terms of our convictions to say, 'You are right,' 'I'm really sorry, I seem not to have been understanding you, please explain to me again ...' will usually have the same effect and lead into radical listening.

FOR REFLECTION

- Review in your mind some escalations you know about, whether of conflict or other problematic processes. Are they symmetrical or complementary?
- Think of a complementary move to cut through the symmetrical ones.
- Think of a symmetrical move to cut through the complementary ones.
- Do you have any examples in mind of this model actually stopping the escalation?

Dealing with dyadic conflict

What should the facilitator do if the attack happens between two group members, or if an angry mini-war happens between two group factions? Open conflict between group members is a problem for which I developed a specific technique in the 1990s; the **dyadic conflict resolution** model. This is a tightly structured technique, as follows:

When you are aware that a difference of opinion is becoming a conflict between two sides, say something like:

'Hang on, let me see if I can understand what's happening here'. Then listen carefully in turn to their stories (slowing down the process, reducing arousal). Block interruptions. Usually;

- A's story is that it's B's fault (B has locus of control)
- B's story is that it's A's fault (A has locus of control).

They want you to judge between them but at all costs **avoid getting into a judging position**.

1. Tell A's story back to A. Check if you are getting it right – summarise.
2. Tell B's story back to B. Check if you are getting it right – summarise.

Externalise – make the problem outside of A & B. For example;

- Define it as a Vicious Circle or Dance ... the more A does the more B does the more A does, describing a circle.
- The more the Anger comes in, the more A ... the more B ...

Then change the pronoun from YOU to WE, for example:

- 'I wonder what **we** can do to break the Vicious Circle?'
- 'I wonder how **we** can make the Anger shrink?'

Wait for suggestions. Accept all ideas uncritically and with enthusiasm. Collect as many ideas as possible from both sides.

Often the first ideas expressed are what the **other** can do.

If A says, 'If only B would ...' accept that as an excellent idea but add, 'That's something B could do. Can you also think of anything **you** could do?' (Locus of control back to self).

Finally discuss how these ideas might be implemented.

It is important to follow the technique exactly. In the first part, if the facilitator tells A's story to B or vice versa it will feel like arguing and the strategy will not work. The change from the second person to the plural first person pronoun is also essential. It turns the warring factions into a problem-solving team. In large group organisational interventions, Bunker and Alban (1997) also emphasise the necessity of this change from the 'I' to the 'we'.

Remember the contrast between conflict and disagreement; whereas disagreement can be extremely useful, conflict, which implies hostility, defensiveness and heightened arousal, is invariably destructive. Some groups might be brought together specifically to address conflict, as in the following example.

Doug is a manager for a team of four women and three men. They have bitter concerns about how he is managing them, and two colleagues who used to be on his team have already left the firm. The team agree that Doug is dictatorial and unable to listen but also realise that he is anxious and driven by organisational quota demands from 'above'. They all find themselves unable to confront him about his style.

Maria is to facilitate a one-off meeting between Doug and his team to resolve this problem. She is anxious that the issues should be made clear but that no one should be penalised or disadvantaged, and that Doug should not become more anxious, leading to a spiral of further dogmatism and conflict. How is she to handle this? She does not want the team members to attack Doug but neither does she want them to back down and minimise the problems.

At the opening of the meeting it becomes apparent that the team members are unable or unwilling to state what their issues are. Maria finds that she has to summarise them, which she does very early, in terms of the emotional shape of the session (give bad news very early – see discussion of the emotional shape of sessions in previous chapter). She can then utilise the team members' non-confrontational style to protect Doug from feeling too attacked and reach the desired outcome of action points to address the issues. In doing this she uses a modification of the dyadic conflict model, starting with the clearest possible statements of the team's and Doug's positions, presenting them as an escalating pattern and then moving to the 'what can WE do to resolve the issues?' phase.

Scapegoating should not occur if the facilitator has followed the principles and techniques we describe but is nevertheless something the facilitator should watch out for and counter if it begins to occur. This can often be done by **commenting on the process**. This is a practice of putting on the table what is happening in the room and then proceeding to be curious about it. Here are some examples.

George, I notice that whenever Brigit talks about the difficulties management has around finances you look angry or anxious. I wonder if I'm right and what that is about?

I feel as though I am getting more and more anxious as we speak. I wonder if any of you share that feeling and what that is about? Or are you feeling quite different?

It seems to me, Hilly and James, as though you are getting into a process of revving each other up, and it's my impression that this happens quite often? Can we explore that, or do you think I've got it wrong?

It seems as though we might all too easily start picking on Moira when she says this. I wonder why? Are we really giving Moira space to have her own opinions or do we have a feeling that she should fall in line with ours?

Group roles seem almost always to be allocated over time. These are not necessarily problematic but again should be a focus of the facilitator's awareness. They actually can be useful but it might equally be useful to engender discussion about them. Ideally, they should not become too fixed as they can lock members into 'thin story' restraints on their potential actions and personal development. Looking at roles can help members wonder whether they also take those roles in other contexts and what are the advantages and pitfalls of doing so. How to make them more flexible if necessary is a content issue but requires process observation to identify.

The person who talks too much

Participants are very varied in how much they talk or participate in the group content. It is essential for facilitators to know how, kindly and without undermining, to partially silence those who take up too much space/time and to draw forth in a safe way the silent participant. Every facilitator needs to know how to interrupt. It is worthwhile to watch the techniques of good TV interviewers, especially when they are dealing with more than one person at a time. They need the same skills.

We mentioned this in the section on bouncing the ball around the room (see above). Bouncing the ball is one way to prevent the conversation from becoming a monologue, as we pick up on what one person is saying and invite comments from the others. But before we pick up we have to interrupt, preferably without wounding the talker. We could, of course, just interrupt, but most of us experience this as being dismissive of what we are saying. There are exceptions to this. The more comfortable the talker is with the facilitator, the better a direct interruption will be tolerated. Some facilitators do this with a physical signal, like holding up a hand as a 'stop' signal. After this we might say something like, 'Yes, thanks, Derek, but let's hear from someone else now'. Even if directly and directively interrupting, if possible it is good to give a signal that we have been listening carefully and respectfully.

Another way to do this is to interrupt with a summary of what the person is saying, make some (positive) comment on it and then turn to invite further comments from the others. Yet another possibility, which also signals radical listening, is to over-speak part of a sentence, weave it into a comment and move on rapidly to someone else.

If the problem persists we might need to name it, framing it kindly and remembering to bounce the ball immediately. We might say something like:

> *Kathy, I love your enthusiasm, but it's important for us to hear what other people are thinking too. Jean, what were you thinking about that?*
>
> *Jerry, you give us such a wealth of ideas, but I worry that other people might be less confident and feel that there is no space for expressing what they are thinking. Mike, do you have anything to add to what Jerry has just said?*

As someone who can easily talk too much myself, I am able to say:

> *Will, you're a bit like me – we get carried away with what we are thinking and it's hard to shut us up! But we often need to rein ourselves in and let some less talkative people tell us their ideas. Let's hear what you others are thinking about this.*

FOR REFLECTION

- Would you say you talk too much or too little?
- Practice interrupting by over-speaking the last sentence. Does it work? Does the person you have interrupted experience you as rude?

Aggression, passive-aggression and assertiveness

We may well bring into a group feelings which don't necessarily belong to the group. Because we are constantly responding to life events and interactions, the fallout of these can enter even the best-run group.

> *Mike has had a bad day topping a terrible week. He arrives at the meeting feeling irritable and soon starts arguing aggressively with what others are saying. It is not easy for the facilitator, Ed, to keep himself from responding aggressively but he manages to do so. However, even his radical listening and non-confrontational response calm Mike only to a certain extent, and some disruption of the group process ensues.*

Meanwhile, Betty has responded with a customary tearfulness and mur-murs to a friend that she is being damaged by the tense atmosphere – a response which puts the group into a double bind. They feel they should meet Betty's needs but are also a bit resentful of her because, yet again, her needs seem so much more powerful than those of any other group member.

In this example, Mike is bringing into the group anger which is generated by other factors. While a group is an open system (and we remember from Chapter 2 that no truly closed social systems exist) it is inevitable that issues from its environment will impinge on occasions. He here reacts to his own general upset by **aggression**.

When we feel under threat we have complex reactions which are partly physiological and partly psychological and which have been developed as habits of reacting over our lifetimes. We have all heard of the **fight or flight** reaction. This is a wonderful design feature of our bodies and is psycho-physiological. When we experience threat there is a release of various hormones (notably epinephrine, otherwise known as adrenalin, but the reaction is much more chemically complex than this) and the **sympathetic nervous system** comes into play. This is part of the **autonomic nervous system**, which regulates non-voluntary muscles and the automatic functioning of our bodies, including our hearts, blood vessels, digestive system, immunological system, urinary system. When we need to be ready for an action which might be needed to save our lives, our bodies move blood to the large muscles, especially in the arms and legs, and away from the viscera and head. Our heart rate increases and our blood pressure rises. Fats and sugars are released into the bloodstream. Our lungs take in more oxygen. Generally, we become stronger, more able to fight or run away, although sometimes the reaction might also produce freeze. The face might pale or become redder, or vary between these and we sweat more. Sometimes, in very extreme sympathetic nervous reactions, we lose sphincter control.

Anger is one of the emotions relating to this sympathetic nervous system reaction. The other one is fear. There are differences between the two emotional reactions but both are 'high arousal' emotions. This means that the automatic responses tend to over-ride our ability to think clearly and calmly. Although this is excellent for survival in really dangerous situations it is obviously not very useful to our general functioning in relationships. Of course, we are also describing an extreme. Mike, in the above example, has only a low arousal reaction so has some control over his anger response. He is not aggressing too openly. It is important to remember that although arousal over-rides cognitive function, this is not an absolute effect except in situations of gravest danger.

Before we interpret what is happening as a threat. No arousal if the interpretation is that the situation is not threatening.	During the reaction, when the others react calmly and soothingly, reducing our arousal. (Aggression from others will intensify the arrousal.)	When we can reflect on our own response, especially with regard to its possible effect on others. In most situations we control our reactions to a certain extent.

TIME ————————————————————————→

Figure 5.2 Points at which to deal with anger response

Mike has many possibilities for modifying his own reaction. The first is in his perception of whatever upset him in the first place. The more he perceived this as attacking or threatening, the stronger his reaction would be. We can see how this relates to Attachment Theory and why people are more likely to become violent in intimate relationships. It is because those relationships are more important emotionally and therefore perceived threats to them will evoke more arousal; the securely attached will have better control than those who are anxiously attached. Once already angry, Mike will still modify his arousal depending on ongoing factors in the environment, especially the social environment. Finally, the more self-awareness he has, the more he will be able to stand outside his own reaction and reflect on it. More conscious control can be developed.

FOR REFLECTION

- If you have a difficult or upsetting time, how are you likely to react? – become angry, tearful, anxious or what?
- What helps you to deal with this reaction so that you can function thoughtfully in relationships?

We mentioned previously the difference between emotions which draw people closer together and those which push them further apart. Emotions are contagious. Anger is divisive because it produces high arousal in the other as well. In the above example, Ed had to use his own cognitive functions to counter his automatic response to Mike's aggression. His own response was thought-out and useful. In training about how to de-escalate violence, we learn that we should never counter aggression with aggression; the same principle applies even if the aggression is at a lower level.

Aggression is anger turned outward in such a way as to be experienced as punishing. It is a display of power, intended to intimidate and control others. There are huge variations in the extent to which different individuals feel and express aggression. Some have had life experiences which have taught them that aggression is a useful stance, giving them power to impose their preferences on others. They are the bullies. The cost of aggression, distancing them from others, is either not perceived, seen as the fault of the other or accepted as a necessary and unimportant trade-off.

Not that Mike is necessarily a bully; he is just inclining towards this response after an upsetting day. There is a continuum of possible responses. But bullies do join groups. Whether the behaviour is frequent or occasional, it is the job of the facilitator to manage it and not to allow it to affect group process. It might become essential to confront Mike, and it can be seen that this requires a careful balancing so that Ed's confrontation is not in itself aggressive. Usually it will be better to deal with the issue on a subsequent occasion when Mike no longer has the contra-reason effect of high arousal controlling him. If necessary, in the worst-case scenario, Mike might have to be asked to remove himself from the group, either temporarily or even permanently.

Betty's response, in contrast with Mike's, is passive-aggressive. She has also learned a way of controlling people, not by aggressing but by occupying a victim position. Passive-aggression is also aggression because it is also a learned behaviour pattern which gives its protagonist social power, although in this case the arousal emotion might look more like fear than anger. Betty does not feel able to counter Mike, but in fact her display of weakness counters him quite effectively (except that it might make him feel still more aggressive). Her behaviour draws people towards her and into her corner at first, but paradoxically is also distancing long-term. Her peers have an uneasy feeling that they are, in fact, being controlled.

Because Betty's story about herself is that she is a victim, Ed's confrontation of her behavioural pattern needs to be even more gentle than his confrontation of Mike's. Nevertheless, he will also have to deal with this because it will also be destructive of group process.

In both cases, the confrontation might take place in or out of the group context, depending on the type of group and its permissions. Ideally, it will be confronted gently over time both in and out of the group.

For all of us, the ideal is for us not to be either aggressive or passive-aggressive but to be assertive. **Assertiveness is the ability firmly to**

express one's own view and hold one's own boundaries without coercion, without a need to aggress or force anyone else. Assertive people do not need to apply power because they feel powerful enough. They feel securely attached. They can express their own views but still have psychological space to listen carefully and respectfully to the views of others.

FOR REFLECTION

- How easy do you find it to be appropriately assertive? If it is difficult for you, you might like to do some assertiveness training (not within the scope of this book).
- How would you describe to someone the difference between assertiveness and aggression? What about passive-aggression?

We have seen that styles of relating are habitual and therefore relatively stable but that they can change over time as we co-construct ourselves in relationship with others. If our relationships in groups or families give us a secure base, we become more securely attached. If we receive interest and respect in an environment which encourages us to respect and enjoy the differences brought in by others who think differently from us, we lose our need for aggression or passive-aggression.

This is an ongoing, life-long process. Unfortunately, the direction of travel might also be the opposite of this. If we are stuck in relationships and groups which undermine us, we are more likely to become defensive, self- rather than other-absorbed and obsessed with keeping up our side against others. In other words, we buy into aggression or passive-aggression.

Another pernicious effect of undermining groups is an over-sensitivity about 'what others think of me'. This excessive self-consciousness is endemic in many modern cultures and is promoted constantly by media absorption with personal image. There is a dominant story that we need to aspire to a normative 'ideal' both in physical terms and in cognitive/psychological qualities. Many powerful industries thrive on these 'ideals'; cosmetics, food, clothing, health products, sports and exercise, music and entertainment – the list is endless. Massive economic forces are opposing our diversity and individual differences. This is an impact of the larger group in which we all live.

Nevertheless, this cultural pressure can be countered in the smaller, more intimate groups we belong to. Our families are obviously the closest and have the strongest impact but our work and social circles are also important.

FOR REFLECTION

- How much are you controlled by what others think of you?
- What experiences might have influenced how this is for you?
- If you are not satisfied with how things are in this regard, what would help your feelings and reactions be more your preferred way of being?

Summary

As a group continues to develop, there are certain factors which will be challenging for the facilitator. Often these relate to conflict or aggression. As we have said from the first chapter of this book, although disagreement is essential, conflict, by our definition, is never useful and it cannot be ignored. Facilitation is not for the faint-hearted. Conflict, aggression and passive-aggression must be confronted and dealt with, while keeping or moving towards a culture of healthy self-assertion by all members. We need all to be increasingly respectful of each other in our diversity, making space for different, even opposite, ideas. The facilitator has the task of moving always in the direction of healthy communication, flattened power hierarchies and radical listening. It is the facilitator's responsibility to ensure that all voices are heard. This chapter has covered some of the principles involved and specific techniques designed to bring them about.

6

PUTTING IT ALL TOGETHER: SOME SAMPLE APPLICATIONS

The family consultation model

Linda, who is 26 and has a diagnosis of psychosis, is a bit bewildered but beginning to feel more hopeful than she has for a long time. She is sitting in a 'family consultation meeting' with her parents, Joy and Bob, and her therapist and care co-ordinator from the mental health team. The facilitator has told her she needs to be 'the captain of the team' as she is the one who is living with the experience of psychosis. To her surprise she has been able to explain some of these experiences and has been listened to with interest. She is the expert on what it feels like to live with this. She has started to define herself as a person with unusual things in her life rather than as a sad, mad reject.

Her mother, Joy, has been very angry and wanted to put in a formal complaint because she thought the mental health team were not doing what they should and they were refusing to talk to her. She is finding this meeting refreshing. She was able to express her anger when she arrived and the facilitator and team members didn't react defensively but heard her out. She then learned a little about the pressures the team were under because of their resourcing difficulties.

The therapist, Dora, has been feeling a bit stuck but is noticing that meeting Linda's family gives her new ideas. She has never met Bob before but notices that when he makes a contribution to the conversation it seems to open up slightly new ways of thinking.

Glenda, the care co-ordinator, felt defensive when she came in and this grew worse as she heard what Joy had to say. However, she was also encouraged to express what was happening from her own perspective and by now she is feeling that they all understand the pressures she is working under and the fact that she really does care about her clients, within the

112

limitations of her context. She is beginning to think that working together with the family will take some pressure off instead of increasing it.

Bob is surprised to find he has a role. It was always Joy who took Linda to her appointments and dealt with the team. He arrived feeling that he had nothing to contribute but finds that his ideas are respected and that even Joy seems surprised and happy at his input.

By the end of the meeting they feel like a single team of different experts. They have thought about the way forward and have some clarity about what each of them can do to work towards Linda's recovery and how they can keep communication lines open. They agree to meet once more with the facilitator, in about six weeks' time, to check on what progress has been made and what new directions are indicated.

This vignette illustrates a single-session 'group therapy' model, which I applied over a number of years in a mental health NHS trust where systemic resources were very scarce. It became imperative to have the greatest possible impact for the greatest possible number of people, so ongoing family therapy was not usually an option. We called this the 'family consultation model'. Actually, there were usually two sessions, because the later single review session was usually included, just to make sure that the process set in place was still on track and people were still comfortable with their roles. The aim of the consultation meeting was to unstick the system and give people a way to move forward as a single team rather than warring factions.

The meeting sounds like a care planning meeting but tends to feel very different, and this is because it is facilitated according to the principles described in this book, rather than being led by a health professional who seems to have the power in the system. Most clients feel that care planning meetings are just where they are told what they have to do, and most families feel marginalised and disrespected. Even the therapist and care co-ordinator are unlikely to have the sense that people appreciate them and know what pressures they work with.

FOR REFLECTION

- In a meeting which you recently attended, were all the stakeholders present or were some excluded?
- How were competing viewpoints managed?
- Did the meeting end with a greater sense of team-ness or with increased hostility?
- Using ideas you have learned from this book, how might you have improved the outcome, had you been the facilitator?

This is an example of the application of the model for groups described in this book. I have used and use the same principles of group facilitation in many different contexts in the past and present. I have worked with organisations. For example, I ran a two-day team-building workshop for a private school in which parents and staff had got into an adversarial stance in respect of each other. I conducted organisational growth/change seminars for Non-Government (Voluntary Sector) Organisations. I have run university (and other) training workshops and professional personal development groups. However, most of my more recent work has been in the field of Mental Health. I also spent some time training Clinical Psychologist colleagues in the Systemic Narrative approach to groups and in this chapter I feature samples of their work.

In this chapter I have included un-rehearsed interviews with people who have been involved in groups run according to the theory base expounded in this book. Because my recent experience has all been in the field of Mental Health services, these applications are rather specifically within that field. However, I believe that you, the reader, will find ways of applying the ideas to your own team, group or classroom.

The supervision group review

In this transcript I have changed the names of the participants and removed some details which were too specific, as the group chose to be anonymous for inclusion in the book. It is a complex team; made up of therapists of various sorts who supply services into a variety of other teams. Professions included from time to time have been: psychologists, art therapists, social workers, occupational therapists, family therapists and nurses. I have offered them a once-a-month supervision of one and a half hours per session for approximately eight years. It has been a semi-open group because of the many changes of staff in the team over the time that it has run.

Because all potential members are very busy professionals, there is seldom a whole-team membership of the supervision group. All come whenever they possibly can, and the group therefore varies in size from four or five to about twelve; I am never sure who will be there. The group was here recorded when only six were present, as some were involved in delivering training and some were on leave.

Margaret: *Well, this group has been going for years and it's had quite a lot of different people come in and out but it's basically remained as a clinical supervision group. What I'm wanting to ask is about your* *experience of the group, what's been important to you, any comments you feel like making. It's changed a number of times over that time. However, my impression is that the central culture of the group has remained very similar.*

Ann: *Yes. The culture has been quite constant. I think the constancy of knowing there's this space for that kind of reflection has been a very helpful part of our team culture …*

Margaret: *So space for reflection has been important, and …?*

Brenda: *And for me, different perspectives. When you've only got your own head or brain to sort of go round and round – well, for me it can be really helpful to think about how somebody else sees a situation, what you're doing … But supportive as well – that's the other thing – to be able to share something …*

Margaret: *Right. Different perspectives, and not feeling alone with problems?*

Cynthia: *I think it's also, not just the different perspectives, well, not just different people giving their views on something but also the different backgrounds and trainings – everyone has a different view or something to say based on their training or their background.*

Margaret: *So having different backgrounds and professions gives it a richness of perspective because you're able to put your ideas alongside the somewhat different ideas of other people?*

Ann: *Having that plurality of approach is really, really helpful.*

Cynthia: *I was just thinking back to last month when Joe came up with the analogy of those geese jumping off the cliff – with your client, Brenda – how if they had not been on the cliff they would all have died but now one or two could potentially reach the bottom – we got to see a different viewpoint of something happening. A difference of analogy to explain something.*

Dora: *Above all, the group is there and regular! Actually, it was one of the things that made me want to be in this team. It feels so important to have something of this nature. It doesn't happen in every team. And even though it can be hard, you just feel, 'I want to work with that, each of us sitting here face to face, I want to sit in that space, not with our files and everything, just with our thoughts and – ourselves, actually'.*

Cynthia: *I think some places are very unlucky not to have this because they can be completely separate from one another, whereas here you get to see everyone – everyone isn't as perfect as you think and they've all got the same problems and you can see them in here, different professions but all having similar problems. Whereas outside I might see someone and listen to the way they talk and think, 'Oh, you really have it all together, you really …' Then you come in here –*

(General laughter)

Cynthia: *You know, 'I've got the same problem!'*

Margaret: *So in some teams people are isolated and their fantasy is, 'Everybody else has got it all together, and here's just me with my worries and concerns and so on?'*

Dora: *Yes.*

Enid: *I really appreciate it. In other teams you just don't have the space and the time. It's so important, and yet it's just not justified in other services.*

Margaret: *So what does it actually add to you as a team member, or to your work – to things that the organisation might say, 'Well yes, it's a useful thing to provide this space every month for a team?'*

Dora: *I think it makes us a group rather than a collection of individuals …*
I remember being in one team a couple of years ago. When I started there I had this image of us being like all hands. If it was a body it was all hands and all arms and there was no centre as such … like everyone was just an arm. There must be some myth where there was a creature that was just lots of limbs.

I remember the key people in there, some of the senior people, I never saw talking to each other! One particular person who had been there for many years never spoke to another person who had been there for many years and was very senior – I never saw them interact. There was something about that that didn't work. And I feel like we're a body here, we've got different parts and even though we have our difficulties we are at least a group and we have the others.

Margaret: *So there's some grounding in that network of relationships?*

Cynthia: *There's a brain and a stomach – all the important bits that help the arms to function and the legs to function.*

Ann: *I think there's a process. Upstairs most of us share office space but we're only staying with our files and we've got our computers but we don't discuss – I was just thinking, I chat to Enid quite a lot but we don't discuss clinical work because we work in very different parts of the team. I think one of the things that really helps my practice is to think about the work that other parts of the service do; so Brenda, you and I have talked together over many years. In Brenda's case, a lot of our clients will one day be her clients. Not necessarily, but that's the path for them. So hearing about what happens at that end is very helpful for me.*

Margaret: *Mm-hm.*

Ann: *Also thinking about the way that Enid's and Joy's Learning Disabilities team use all sorts of creative communication tools because their assumption is – and has to be – that their clients don't communicate with words; and in fact many of our clients also don't* communicate with words. They could choose to do that – they've got the physical capacity to do that, but they don't. So I think sharing that is, for me, it's been really, really rich, because you don't necessarily get that, outside this context.

Margaret: *It broadens out your practice, instead of narrowing it down?*

Ann: *Yes, that's been my experience.*

Enid: *For us it's the same as well, because obviously you are all working with complex attachment issues and in our team as well, I think if we weren't sat within this team we would look at the children we work with maybe in a slightly different way but now we do have a focus on attachment as well. I think a lot of it is because we are discussing within this wider team.*

Brenda: *I think that's for me too, working with the older ones, thinking about why they can or can't do things and thinking about what happened before …*

Margaret: *If I can get back to the team process, I wonder if anyone can be at all descriptive of what you see as the culture of this team as opposed to other teams? You've said something about it; you've said there's team-ness. And also what you think we've done in this space that has moved that culture in one way or another?*

Dora: *Yeah … I think vulnerability comes to my mind …*

Margaret: *Okay? Just expand on that a bit.*

Dora: *It's something about us … Our clients rely on a secure base and we try to establish that. There's something about us needing to think about that for ourselves and our own vulnerability – I feel vulnerable in this group, sometimes, and I think in a way that's important. I'm glad and grateful to be in touch with the vulnerability that I feel – not just hide it away. So in this space I'm faced with that. It makes me aware that it's not always just me, that it's a shared thing – something about that which keeps alive the connection with each other and the importance of each other.*

Cynthia: *Something else – this space sometimes brings up honesty in how we feel about one another. I think it happened a few months ago when we were talking about the open-plan office. You know, how if you're wanting to do some work and you've got your earphones in and that 'do not disturb' sign has gone up and you want to get on with it. And to bring that in here and say, rather than worrying about it, what does it mean, do others not want to talk to me or …?*

Margaret: *Right. A place that you can be very clear what the dynamics are, even –*

Cynthia: *How we operate outside this supervision group. We can discuss that – it's safe enough to bring that up and not feel – well, feel bad* *about it. So we can say something that you normally wouldn't want to say outside of this space ...*

Dora: *The hard bit for me is that I don't know what I think constructive use of the supervision time is. It feels like it's a spectrum between things about, 'I felt like that when you didn't notice that I needed the desk,' to something very clearly clinical supervision, like talking about that case last time. And I think, 'Oh, are we looking at cases or our process and what do I think is right, what do I need, what do other people think or need?' And sometimes when you come in and say, 'Right, we're going to do a case,' I think, 'Oh, today was when I was a bit more wanting to look at the team'.*

And then sometimes I thought, 'Oh, that's really good, I'm glad we did a case, because I didn't really want to go into that side of things.'

Margaret: *Is there a way of getting a consensus about that, or are we just going to have to stay floaty with that one?*

Fiona: *We kind of do check it out at the beginning but we don't explicitly go, 'What's at the top of the list for people?'*

Ann: *I think everyone knows that there's that spectrum and for me over time I've had to take responsibility for deciding what to say and what not to say, and other people do the same. I used to think, 'Oh, I can't say that because that will upset somebody else'. Actually, a group like this can't work effectively if everybody is too busy thinking about everybody else in that way. We've got – we won't say unkind or insensitive things – we try not to – but at the same time if you just try to double-think – I could easily double-guess you wrong. If you – like last time Dora wanted to talk about a case so I'll say, 'Let's talk about a case,' and then maybe – it doesn't work.*

Margaret: *So you've learned that you all have to speak for yourselves ...*
Is there anything vital that should still be said?

Fiona: *Just that I've found it helpful to say that, to realise that. There isn't a right way of doing it other than perhaps taking responsibility for myself.*

Margaret: *Which I think is happening quite a lot here.*

Fiona: *We're in the profession of thinking about other people, aren't we? So we're always thinking about other people because that's the profession we've got into. We're not in a profession of thinking just about ourselves.*

Margaret: *Yes, but I think that that doesn't mean that you shouldn't be speaking for yourselves, standing up for what you want. That's something that we want for our clients so that's something we should be doing for ourselves as well. It goes back to that vulnerability thing as well.*

Enid: *I think a lot of people have difficulty because of lack of experience of reflective space. So when we check in and go round the room I always pick something I think people won't want to talk about –*
> *(laughter)*

Enid: *Because I'm quite new …*

At this point in the conversation we switched off the recording, though the discussion continued. Enid's final comments show 'warts and all' in that she clearly hadn't been confident in previous discussions. (Laughter in this group signifies general assent that others recognise that feeling.) However, we see a process development here in that Enid is now able to label her lack of confidence and bring it to the group for acceptance and support.

FOR REFLECTION

- Are you ever a participant in a group supervision? What do you personally feel you need from the group?
- If you are a supervisor, would a group format help or hinder the tasks of the supervision?
- How would you create a 'safe space' if supervising or leading a group or team?

The training course for carers of people with serious mental health problems

For some time I ran a series of carers' trainings for anyone caring for a person with serious mental health problems, including depression, anxiety, psychosis, eating disorders, the so-called personality disorders. Participants were usually the parents of the patient but spouses and children of the patient were also included. The most recent one I ran, which we named, 'Living with Psychosis', was for that diagnosis only but did include the client/patient as well as the carers and some of the mental health team, which fitted better with my own model of inclusiveness.

These trainings comprised four sessions of two hours at a time, run on an evening, a month apart. As always, the strength of the group was in the diversity and mutual support, even though there was theoretical input as well, as is reflected in the following comments from participants.

It would be so helpful if all carers caring for a person with a mental health condition could be offered this course. The diversity of the group moves the course and it is applicable to all, no matter where they are on their journey. We learn from each other and we learn more about ourselves. I feel more relaxed and I have reassessed my coping strategies – thank you.

The following description was written by Jill Scholl, an associate lecturer in Social Work and herself a carer, who attended one of the earlier courses. Therefore, the one she describes included only carers but a variety of diagnoses.

When we met the first time, and we introduced ourselves, and said a little about ourselves, it was clear we represented a wide range of age groups and a diverse range of caring roles. The majority of us were mothers with caring responsibilities for our sons or daughters. Margaret used a flip chart to ask us what we wanted from the course.

This was clearly helpful to get this list on to a sheet of paper, but whereas the other carers seemed to have clear ideas of what they wanted, I was a little hesitant to offer my suggestions; these were 'maintaining hope', 'accepting a poor quality of life'. They seemed rather depressing, although I view myself as optimistic, however a realist. The suggestions from the other carers were around dealing with violence, boundaries and coping, they were more directly associated with managing the caring role.

Margaret did a couple of icebreakers during the first week, and explained the systems basics. She talked about externalising and symmetrical and complementary escalation. Fortunately for me, she put these on a handout and gave them to us the following meeting. I found these interesting but hard to put into context at the first meeting. I was quickly distracted when members of the group spoke of their own experiences.

I had given the question of 'what we want from the course' some considerable thought before the first meeting. I was looking for some sort of validation that I had managed my caring role with my eldest son OK. At 49, he was considerably older than the other carers' children; he had a very late diagnosis of chronic paranoid schizophrenia in his mid-30s. It had taken a further 10 years to find a regime that suited him, and gave him a level of social inclusion that he could manage. We have now had a welcome four years of relative calm, after 20 years of difficulties. I am left wondering had I done enough? Should he be in a better place?

I had even thought about my childhood. I was the youngest of three and my mother also had schizophrenia, although this was not diagnosed until she was in her 50s. She came to the attention of Health and Social

Services after she had attempted suicide. I found it hard to separate myself from my mother; she was very controlling. As a child I fitted in with her beliefs, to keep the peace, but as I grew older I had to learn to stand up for myself, to choose my own friends and live my own life. I needed to put some space between us, and keep her at arms distance. After she was diagnosed and I realised the difficulties she had faced for so much of her life, I felt very sad for her. I suppose I was a carer for her too in a way. Had I done enough?

It was, I think, the second meeting when Margaret asked us to write down a list of 'what is the point of someone's life?' These could be shared with the group afterwards if we wanted. The next thing she asked us to write down was 'what things has our son/daughter/wife/husband taught us?' I remember thinking for a moment before writing my list. I noticed the other carers did not seem to be writing much on this topic. When Margaret asked if anybody wanted to share their list, there were few takers, and so I read out my list.

- Taught me how brave and loyal he is
- Taught me there is always time for humour
- Reminded me he can still be insightful at times
- Taught me it's OK to be different
- Taught me it's OK to have a family member who is mentally ill
- Taught me to 'take on' Health and Social Services

The last one raised quite a bit of laughter!

I realised then that the carers in our group were all at different stages of our 'journey', and as the oldest carer, it made sense that I was probably further along. This did not mean I would not get as much from the course, but my needs might be slightly different.

My relationship with my son was good, compared with the other carers, although this had not always been the case. There had been times when I knew he really did not like or trust me and I had been quite frightened of his behaviour at times. I found that our relationship improved after I asked him to move, four years ago. I had been driven to this decision, but was still full of fear that this would be reason enough for him to walk out of my life. I shared this with the group. It helped me to recall this defining decision.

My son lives on the fringe of society, wears dark glasses and a hat all the time. However, he manages his own finances, owns a car, and rents a council flat. He visits me most weeks and we have a meal together every weekend. He has no insight into his illness, and I am excluded from his care plan because he does not wish to have his 'illness' discussed with me, *he wanted confidentiality. I shared this with the group, and found this was quite comforting to some of the carers there with similar circumstances. It was comforting for me to know they understood what I was saying.*

My concerns about how well I had managed my relationships with my mother and my son were laid to rest when other carers in the group sought answers to their current problems. I learned that the boundaries I had put in place were, in fact, OK, and necessary. Living with a loved one who has a mental illness can make impossible demands of the family. I used to say 'it is not his fault, it is his illness', which is true but can be an unrealistic burden – there was a pivotal moment when I needed to say that I could not be drawn into his illness with him. I was better placed, for all concerned, at a safer distance, with a boundary that I was comfortable with.

My relationship with my son is currently good. I have endeavoured to see his life through his eyes, and understand why he seems content. I cannot help being a little sad that his medication, and, perhaps his illness has taken away his confidence, and that even small tasks that he used to do and enjoy are now out of his reach. But we look at the jobs around the farm together and I work alongside him to complete the task. I have to remind my other son that he should not be dismissive of his older brother's attempts to join in on our conversations about work or holidays. He has nothing current to add to our conversation, and instead refers to things that happened to him 20 years ago, before his illness.

It was at the third week, when a few less carers had been able to attend. The day of the week had to be changed due to the availability of the room and I felt a real bonding in the group, which was good. We had always been respectful of each other, and sensitive to the need to be heard; now the carers were gaining confidence about sharing and challenging.

I realised during the course that my stress came from my relationship, or lack of relationship, with medical staff involved in the care and support of my son. They exclude me because of his decision around confidentiality. He says he is afraid that I may say something, unintentionally, that could lead to him being hospitalised again. He does not trust the workers, or their motives. He has no insight into his illness. I would like to explain this to them, and it frustrates me that we cannot work together for his good. I need to reconsider these relationships and ask myself what they can actually add to the quality of my son's life. If there is something tangible, then I need to renegotiate my position with them. If I can think of nothing, then I can stop thinking I have fallen short of my responsibilities as a parent/carer.

Margaret facilitates a group of carers to work through the things that matter to them. There were times that we worked in pairs, and sometimes in small groups, but mostly we worked as a large group, which suggests an element of trust between us. I have always found working with other carers helpful, and with a good facilitator this can have positive outcomes for all, no matter where you are on your journey.

FOR REFLECTION

- Why did this experienced and professional carer need the group?
- Reading her account, what techniques and ideas from this book can you identify?

The mental health inpatient ward open patients' group

Here follows an interview with Dr Tom Smiley, who for nine years had been running an open inpatient therapeutic group. He had had previous training in group analysis but then trained with me in the systemic narrative approach to groups and used this theory base for the group which he here describes.

Patient details are fictionalised, as in the vignettes of the rest of the book, to protect confidentiality. We can see here the principle of self-selection, interestingly in what might be considered the most difficult of circumstances, as the group members were suffering from acute episodes of mental illness at the time.

Margaret: *Do you want to just start with a general description of the group, who used to come, how it worked?*

Tom: *Yes, first of all it was weekly and then it became more or less daily, about three or four times a week. The group was supposed to run for 45 minutes but it really varied. Sometimes it would only be about half an hour, sometimes it would run for an hour and a half, if there was really something important going on. It was a clinical decision.*

Margaret: *Okay so, what would happen in the group, how would you start it?*

Tom: *Well, we would advertise it every morning and go around inviting people. It was a totally open invitation; it was announced every morning in the community meeting after breakfast. Anyone could request to come but we would also go around asking the individuals we thought would benefit. Also the consultants and nurses would recommend it to people as part of their treatment. We occasionally excluded people if there were too many people with mania in the group or if someone we*

123

thought was being too aggressive on the ward. It was quite rare that we had to exclude somebody.

Margaret: *So literally anybody came? They self-selected largely, although it might have been suggested by someone that they should come?*

Tom: *Yes.*

Margaret: *How many would come?*

Tom: *It would be between two and about 11 people; max was probably 11 or 12. Some days it would be all new people and other days it would be people who had been consistently coming through the week so it looked very different. It looked different according to the type of person who came in, what their difficulties were. And different according to who'd been before and who hadn't, as you can imagine.*

Margaret: *Right, so there were a lot of things that were variables. One would be how many people were there, one would be were they new or had they been before, were they following up on stuff they had talked about previously in the group, and so on ... I'd like you to describe a group, just thinking about one of those days when there were three or four people and how that was, and then a day when you had quite a big group and how that went.*

Tom: *That's a big and diverse group. Yes, just hearing you say that, there were a lot of different variables. That was one of the main features of that type of work compared to the group analysis groups I've been in, when you knew exactly who was going to be sitting in which seat every week for a whole year.*

Margaret: *Right.*

Tom: *It's the total opposite on an in-patient open group. You can't predict that anybody would be anywhere or that they'd ever come back again. So that means that every group has got to function as a one-off group that can get somewhere on its own. You don't assume that you'll have the next day to follow anything up. But it also means that you can start a process which hopefully will continue with some of the people outside the group time.*

At first I was rather bewildered with all those variables and whether you could do two things at once. By the time I'd finished after nearly nine years of doing that, I was completely convinced that you could. We had a lot of different processes going on at once in many of the groups. We'd have some kind of group process that was ongoing over several weeks where people became happy with each other and begun to trust each other and care for each other and help each other. But we also had the ones who would just go once; we would do mini interventions in that group just for them, or they would observe what was going on in the wider process and benefit from that. So I never felt, 'Oh dear I wish that person hadn't been there,' or, 'What a waste of time!' There were occasional times when we didn't seem to have got anywhere but that was only about twice a year.

Margaret: *But you couldn't know who were the people you needed to do a mini intervention with, because you couldn't know who was going to be there tomorrow. They might even be discharged by tomorrow.*

Tom: *Yes exactly, that was one of the reasons the group was exciting and challenging and clinically demanding and stimulating. You had to draw on your skills and experience very quickly in a way you couldn't predict each morning.*

Margaret: *Give us a picture of a group then? A more or less four people group.*

Tom: *Okay, well I normally had a nursing staff member with me too, or a peer support member. They were very helpful since they had been through the mental health system themselves. So it would normally be me and one, or maybe two, other staff. And if there were say just two or three patients in there who had been before, or say two who had been before and it had that sense of continuity and steadiness, we might take up on something from the previous session, take it and turn it in to something deeper.*

We'd start off, as I always started, by doing some very quick ground rules, mostly to do with confidentiality and 'feel free to leave if you want to' and 'this isn't compulsory' and that kind of thing. And then I would gauge whether they needed to introduce themselves to each other and I would introduce myself and the staff if necessary. I would then start with the question, 'Is there anything anybody had wanted to bring up today in the group? Anything anyone wanted to talk about?'

Often there would be no response to that. They'd just say no, so I would try and work out an advantageous way to open. Sometimes this would be, 'We talked about this yesterday, has anyone had any reflection?' It would be likely to be that kind of introduction in the smaller group, or straight in there with, 'David you were saying yesterday you were struggling with suicidal thoughts and you wanted to talk a bit more about that today – shall we kick off with that?' When everyone's in crisis and you're in that in-patient setting you can be really direct.

And then if it was David talking, then he would say a little bit more and I would try and keep out of it. It was a mixture for me, as I would try to keep out of it where I thought other patients needed to talk and share their own strategies and connect. But I also felt I was someone there with expertise who might have something useful to contribute to each individual situation, so I would do mini interventions one-to-one across the room, with the others watching it, almost as an outsider witnessing sort of thing. Which actually developed as a process that worked very well for us that we got more and more into.

Margaret: *So you would be having a conversation with, say, David, who was suicidal, and the rest of the group would be there observing but then also joining in.*

Tom: *Yes, sometimes. And I would leave it to them, I think. So if they wanted to come back to David and give him some reassurance or sympathy that would be great and it's just so much more powerful in terms of patients connecting with each other and helping each other than in a case review meeting where all the professionals are trying to do it. It's a little bit like being in the patients' sitting room and they're pouring their heart out and they've got like-minded people around them who know how they're feeling and can come up to them and give them a hug. So I really try to facilitate an environment where patients could connect emotionally with each other in that way.*

But there were many times where it seemed to be that a moment had come up where the professional was going to talk one-to-one with the patient and the others wanted that. It wasn't because other people had run out of things to say, but it just seemed to be that it was right for the moment. It would generally last a few minutes. We would have what I suppose was similar to a one-to-one therapy discussion with other people watching and then feeding back afterwards.

It then often would become a sort of psycho-educational setting where I could teach the others as well and then generate an interesting discussion. Or it would be a little more systemic and I would ask more about the support groups around the patient when they were at home, often with a question like, 'What can you expect when you go back home and is there anything you'll need at home if you're going to sustain the great progress you've been making here?'

Or we would get right in to their childhood, not in a totally intense, interpretative type of way, but more, 'So you were neglected by your parents and now you fear abandonment?' for example. 'So there's a very strong connection there, it's not your fault.' People would often disclose a bit of trauma and sometimes want to talk about it and then the others could again gather around them a bit for support, or disclose their own pasts and we'd have a very, very powerful half hour sitting with quite heavy material from peoples' pasts.

Margaret: *So the picture I'm getting is, even though it was an open group, maybe partly because it was an in-patient ward, the group itself made a really strong containing environment?*

Tom: *Yes usually it did. Very rarely it wouldn't, because there were too many psychotic people in the room or someone was too aggressive and* *would try picking on somebody who would say something they didn't like. So there were occasions when I had to be very careful to manage it.*

Margaret: *How did you manage it? Let's say it's a really good group that's going great, but now you've got one person picking on someone else, what did you do with that kind of stuff?*

Tom: *Well, a range, from have a constant signal like putting my hand up if someone with a known manic episode kept butting in. I generally found that there was a way of getting them to be quiet consistently, either putting my hand up or just keep on saying, 'Please be quiet, John, so and so is trying to talk,' and having to say that time after time, it ranged from that ...*

Margaret: *Being very direct about it, but accepting, so people didn't feel threatened, they just felt, 'That's okay, I need to try to remember to be quiet' –*

Tom: *Exactly, and often it was them just remembering and it would go from there through asking someone to leave, asking a fellow staff member to take them out and saying, 'This isn't working, having you here today, thank you for joining us but let's try again tomorrow.' Then I would try to follow them up afterwards in case they were feeling a bit miffed, but they wouldn't normally. They generally knew what was going on, or someone else had told them they were being irritating and they needed to be quiet.*

Margaret: *Did you find that actually if there was a difficult dynamic that the group usually dealt with it? 'John you're being a bit aggressive now, why don't you just be quiet?' from one of the group members?*

Tom: *Yes, that definitely happened, that's the ideal isn't it? Sometimes people's illnesses very much threw chaotic dynamics into the room. Once or twice this was not conducive to continuing the group, but it was very rare.*

Margaret: *It's interesting that it was so rare though. What you're talking about, in terms of dynamics, would be considered the worst case scenario. You've got acutely ill people!*

Tell me now about if the group was big? You've described a small group, although we've gone into some more general things, like what do you do about difficult dynamics, but how was it different if 11 people were there?

Tom: *Umm ... If there were that many people there would often be a lot of new people and I'd try and pay particular attention to the new people. I needed to work out whether they wanted to sit there and just listen. That was perfectly acceptable; that's one of the ground rules. I say, 'You don't have to talk.'*

Margaret: *Right.*

Tom: ... *Or whether they're getting agitated. You can generally tell if someone's getting agitated because they had something to say and somebody else is hogging the limelight. I would then try and find a moment to stop whoever was talking a lot and directly bring somebody in who looked as if they wanted to talk.*

Margaret: *So your job was to watch and see who might want to be talking ...*

Tom: *Yes, lots of watching. I had to try and be aware of everybody. It was quite tricky sometimes. I would position myself in the circle so that I could have a good view of everybody.*

Margaret: *Right.*

Tom: *The key thing I found with the newcomers was to get other, older-timers, to explain that settling in to the ward happened gradually and was quite an intense experience, but you get there in the end. I normally didn't have to say that because I could say to David or somebody, 'What was it like for you settling in? Just remind me because I think you were pretty stressed out when you came in.' Generally I'd have some sense of how everybody had been when they had come in. Often I'd know a lot from the nurses already. Sometimes it would be enough to say, 'When you came in, within 10 minutes you were on the floor of the communal ward area in complete distress and now here you are, sharing your own resources, after three or four weeks, about how to get back on your feet and work towards your discharge.'*

So in the larger group I would try and get people who were new to say something, and it would so often be along the lines of, 'I'm scared, I don't know why I'm here, I don't want to be here, this place is really weird, I'm never going to settle in,' and very quickly other people could be encouraged to say that it was like that for them, just give it a few days ... I didn't even need to say anything.

Margaret: *Your group must have been useful in settling people because, again, the group is acting as a holding place and a vessel for hope. 'Yes it feels awful now, but it's not going to feel awful and there are going to be ways that you can get well and get yourself out of here.'*

Tom: *Yes, promoting hope would be one of the big themes. Every time we were trying to promote some hope.*

Margaret: *So that would be one of your aims, for people to get out feeling stronger, a bit more hopeful?*

Tom: *Definitely, because they can be in places of shattered hope, so yes, there was always a sense that in that room we could increase people's hope, even in one session. Not always, but it was one of the satisfactions of working in that way to find you could directly work on hope.*

Building community was another one. Making the connections happen in the room.

That is a very powerful, specific process that would suddenly start happening. I would see it coming and get with it and connect those two people up who hadn't yet spoken to each other and who had both had children taken away from them or something, and one was way ahead in recovery than the other one. Or someone who had had a psychotic episode and was going to be discharged in a few weeks and was nearly back on his feet. Then this poor new chap who had come in yesterday and was absolutely all over the place. Connecting the two was almost the most important thing I could do.

Margaret: *So they then supported each other for the rest of the day, or the rest of the week?*

Tom: *Often that happened yes. We could get a community going in the room, which didn't seem to be happening on a ward all that easily. There was something about being in that room with a professional in charge and guiding it, that enabled a supportive group socialising process to happen very quickly which could continue outside. It was often surprising how, without it having happened already after they'd been there a week, it happened within half an hour in a room in this sort of group.*

Margaret: *Just to ask about something that I remember way back, when you started doing those groups. There was a concern about people getting into the really dangerous topics like suicide, whether I should actually kill myself, and of you getting into those. How did that work? How was it not dangerous to be dangerous?*

Tom: *Well that turned into two things. One was the original suicide or not suicide question and then we had a more interesting theme of, is there a depth to which you can or really shouldn't go in a group? That was a more intelligent sort of question. Because with the suicide one it was obvious very quickly that people needed to talk about wanting to die and having dark thoughts and they felt they couldn't in most other places on the ward. Very experienced nurses had no problem talking about that at all and did a brilliant service one-to-one, but often the patients felt like they shouldn't bring it up in the communal area or even in ward rounds. In a group with a real sense of safety they were able to bring it up and it didn't increase their risk.*

That's slightly different to the traumatic background, PTSD, that came to the floor quite a bit later actually as we got into more depth in the groups. I suppose as I got better at helping people talk I realised that I should be helping them to talk up to a point but probably not allowing them to talk past a certain point, if you see what I mean.

Margaret: *Not letting people go into memories which they're not going to be able to handle, which you wouldn't do individually either –*

Tom: *That's right. It's such a specific clinical skill, I think, to visually see when somebody might be going back into the past, you know, on the edge of having a flashback. And they may have just come on to the ward and just be talking about how they're settling in and suddenly they're going in to the background and you have to say at that point, 'Hold it, things will get worse if we go down that route.'*

Margaret: *You would say that in the group?*

Tom: *'Now isn't the time'. And sometimes I would gauge it from the other patients too. They would not like it. I would have to say, 'Now is probably not the time to talk about the abuse you went through as a child.' I had to halt that process very quickly.*

Margaret: *So you would halt that process by directly saying, 'I don't think we should talk about that now'? Did you have other ways of halting that process as well in the group? Or did the group halt it sometimes?*

Tom: *Quite often people in the group would say, 'I'm not comfortable talking about this,' and I hadn't realised that they had been abused.*

Margaret: *So people felt as though they could be quite open about, 'This isn't comfortable for me, I can't go there '*

Tom: *Yes, patients were often very good at saying that, and they said it before I did. I think as time went on we saw more trauma on the ward.*

Margaret: *Right. But in terms of the group dynamics, if anything, over the nine years you saw an improvement in the group itself being able to create community and that sort of thing?*

Tom: *Yes.*

Margaret: *Is there anything else that you think we haven't talked about, that you think was really important?*

Tom: *Well there are some themes that come to mind when I think about the group. Things like deconstructing peoples' problem-based stories. I think a lot of that was done by the group.*

And they fairly naturally did outsider witnessing because I could literally, if it was a fairly mature group, turn to another person who'd been silent for five minutes and say, 'Having known David for two weeks now and been on the ward with him, what are your reflections on what he said about his past and how he's progressing?' and I'd get some amazing things that I could not have matched in terms of therapeutic power.

Margaret: *Right.*

Tom: *Those were absolutely beautiful groups. We had those about every fortnight and I came out of some of those groups thinking, 'What happened there was so wonderful because we had this mix of patients who* *were intelligent enough or thoughtful enough to reflect about each oth-er's issues'. That could have never been achieved in a one-to-one therapy session if it was just me and them. A kind of outsider witnessing.*

I would pick someone who I knew was a fairly good judge of charac-ter, or a staff member and say, 'We've just heard from so and so a few moments ago about how miserable they are and how they're making no progress. I know you don't know each other very well but could you just give us your take on how they have been doing, because you were there when they came in and you're there now.'

*Of course I'd only ask them if I thought something hopeful was com-ing. They would invariably say, 'Yes, he came in and he didn't want to talk to anybody and he was actually quite grumpy and shouted at me,' or whatever. 'And since then we've been sitting at a table reading a newspaper and I've found out that he's a really good guy! We didn't realise that at first and now the three of us have been going out for a smoke together and having a real laugh. He always says how unhappy he is but he's made **us** really happy.' I mean we literally had people word for word saying, 'This person here, they don't realise it, but they have made my stay here worthwhile.'*

Margaret: *So you had that real Catharsis thing ... 'We got moved on by what this person said or did.'*

Tom: *Yeah, it was really amazing sometimes. And you could see some-times patients sitting there with their mouth hanging open thinking, 'I cannot believe someone who's not a professional is saying I'm valu-able!' and that was really special.*

So there was that theme and that developed. I couldn't do that at the beginning nine years ago, I don't think. My thoughts were totally taken up by trying to figure out who should speak next and should they or shouldn't they talk about wanting to die, but by the end I had enough sort of forward thinking space. I could attend to the fact that so and so over here hadn't said anything and might have something really valu-able to say to the miserable person in the corner.

Margaret: *Okay.*

Tom: *Working with nursing staff was brilliant because they have a whole different position regarding the system and anything to do with the procedures or how the ward works. They were often my co-facilitators. They're there on the ground all day long and they are fantastic third party commentators or outside witnesses, able to say, 'Well, when you came in you didn't say anything for three days and now you've had visits from your family and they're supporting you. You've been think-ing about getting a job and things are really looking up. You're really doing well, so don't be so hard on yourself.' Information that I might* *not know. Or, on the sort of more challenging side they'd be able to say, 'Actually, you've said that you're doing really well and there are no problems but yesterday you were really rude to so and so and that does need looking at.' Sometimes it was absolutely perfect when some-one needed a really good challenge because they were pretending that everything was fine and they were brushing things under the carpet and they'd cause problems in the community and the ward.*

Margaret: *So did that then become a focus or a tension in the group? Would you pick up on that?*

Tom: *Yes we had very powerful times where everyone was united that somebody was not being very truthful and the person was able to hear it because it was either a well-established nurse saying it, who they had respect for, or it was another patient. We could work with it. And you could just not let it come up if you thought it would lead to a fight or whatever.*

Margaret: *Right, okay.*

Tom: *So there was so much power in the roles and the positions that even the fact that everyone's length of stay was different and some had just come in and some hadn't – there was real power in that.*

Margaret: *So the variations in themselves created the power that made the group work?*

Tom: *Yeah. You lose some things that in a year-long group you'd get. People that would come to know each other intimately and could chal-lenge each other on their very good knowledge about each other – you don't have that to the same extent, but you've got people who had just been through what a new person is currently going through, which you wouldn't have if everyone was exactly the same. So you lose something. What you gain is probably less commonly realised and talked about. You gain a huge amount I think. If you're brave enough to let processes unfold and nip them in the bud if something slightly less helpful is happening, but just let it flourish if it's something good but you're not quite sure what is unfolding.*

Margaret: *Right, so relaxing with it really.*

Tom: *Yeah.*

Margaret: *Relaxing with the process but being very watching at the same time.*

Tom: *Yes, that suited the way I work, I think.*

Margaret: *Okay, shall we end there? Thanks.*

This description is really interesting, not only because it is of what might be seen as the most difficult possible of therapeutic groups but also because Tom describes something of his own journey as facilitator;

how greater confidence resulted in greater efficacy over time. We are clearly pointed in his description to where our efforts at control must lie in facilitating. We do not have to control the group members or their input, but we do have to trust it and we do have to watch the process carefully to ensure that dynamics remain healthy.

FOR REFLECTION

- Tom alludes to very many of the principles and techniques described in this book. Go through his account again and try to list them.
- To what extent would the ideas expressed here apply equally in a group you know?
- What do you think helped him to gain confidence as a facilitator? What would help you?

The organisational team debrief after serious untoward incidents

The following interview is with another clinical psychologist who was trained by me in the Systemic Narrative approach. She here describes her work in facilitating debriefing meetings after serious incidents in a mental health trust, especially deaths of patients. Jules (not her real name) also runs supervision groups and an open therapy group using the systemic narrative model. The therapy groups are in the community, in contrast with Tom's. We have not included in the book a description of those, though we do refer to the therapy group during this conversation. The debrief model shows a more organisational application.

Margaret: *Would you like to just quickly summarise what the trust decided to set in place with the debriefing and who does what, when?*

Jules: *Yes. I think that about five years ago from a proposal from a colleague there was a policy to offer what was called a 'debrief meeting' to teams who had been working with somebody who had then killed themselves. This is a group support exercise with voluntary attendance, not an individual intervention to treat trauma, in accordance with the international literature base on Critical Incident Stress Management. Usually the debrief is offered for a death. It is now compulsory to do that but now it is widened so you could have a debrief for any other type of* *serious incident, like a staff member being attacked or somebody harming themselves significantly and staff being involved.*

Margaret: *So it's compulsory to offer one now for a death you said?*

Jules: *Yes, and since that it's widened to include all serious untoward incidents. But a debrief should be offered for every single time somebody dies.*

Margaret: *Right. Okay and you would be one of the people who would facilitate a debrief?*

Jules: *Yes.*

Margaret: *Which happens how soon after the event? And what are the events leading up to it?*

Jules: *It's recommended that straight after the event, on the day that the team finds out, there's a defusing event run by the manager, who gathers everyone and checks out everyone's okay and everyone knows generally what happened. People are given the opportunity to seek other conversations or support if they need to and are told there will be a debrief for the team in approximately two weeks. It's recommended that the debrief happens between two or three weeks after the event.*

Margaret: *And that's based on research isn't it? On trauma research which shows this is the best time to do it?*

Jules: *That's right, yes.*

Margaret: *And that's when your involvement usually comes in, because you would be a facilitator for some of those debriefs?*

Jules: *Yes, I would be a facilitator for some of those debriefs. We have a fairly clear model for those meetings, which is a structure by which to ask the team about the incident, ask them about their experience with the incident, think about the person who has died then move on to how the team and individuals are coping with that and whether they need any more support.*

We do have a clear structure but a narrative model helps with the facilitation of that structure, the way in which questions are asked by the facilitator, the way in which people are invited to be involved, to have differences of opinion, to offer their experiences and to pull together. When people come into a room for a debrief they often feel quite nervous and the atmosphere is often very heavy. People appear a bit fragmented and separate from each other. I find that the model seems to pull people together so that even if they have differences of opinion on very sensitive matters there is a common ground about all working together in an extremely difficult atmosphere, and the people have a common goal in terms of why they chose to work in mental health or who they're working with or what their purpose was. A reminder of that is useful.

Margaret: *So it's sort of an opportunity for bringing people together, which I think is a really important part of the model; being able to bring people together on the basis of values which they share.*

Jules: *Yes, and I think when a death occurs it can badly isolate people and people can isolate themselves. You know, a common reaction, 'Did I do the right thing? Am I good at my job? What will other people think of me? Will I be blamed? I'm under scrutiny.' So it's very exposing to come to a debrief anyway. The narrative model seems to really help in re-engaging people with their work and their team, the wider structures around them and the support structures around them, as opposed to them being isolated people.*

Margaret: *So, in summary, what happens with the traumatic experience is that it actually splits people apart in a way. It's a little bit like an explosion.*

Jules: *Yes.*

Margaret: *And everybody lands up in his or her own corner being very prickly and defensive and stressed and feeling blamed and possibly blaming ...*

Jules: *Yes, and it's very difficult for people outside of the debrief often to ask each other even about the facts of the event because people don't want to upset each other or say the wrong thing or they don't know what they should know or what they shouldn't know about the facts of the event, let alone how they or other people feel about it or why someone is off sick or if they are, or if they're just not on shift, or how people are. So the debrief is a real coming together and sharing. Things like bouncing the ball around the room or inviting people at the beginning to give more factual descriptions, being clear that we will have different ideas, seems to bring people together more and make people feel more confident about sharing. Things are normalised and people's reactions can be valued, understood and normalised in quite a sensitive context.*

Margaret: *Do you find the same sort of thing as in your therapy group, of the group actually doing the kindness, doing the love, doing the looking after people who are feeling particularly upset or vulnerable?*

Jules: *A little bit but not as much. I think that people do come in very defensive and in that position quite inwardly focused and not so able to think about looking after other people in the room. Usually, the people in the room who are less close to the incident are able to do more of that, so that's why it's so important that the whole team come and not just the people who were directly involved in the incident. Because you find it's a bit like an onion, where the people who aren't really emotionally affected by the incident but work with the team members who are, are able to do much more of the summarising, the kindness, the, 'I've experienced this before.'*

Margaret: *The less involved look after the people who have been most traumatised by the event?*

Jules: *Yes. The people who have been most traumatised are much less able to do that and are much more focused on their own exposure and safety. They can't really do that for other people but that works quite well, because the more people you have in the room the more that person can kind of relax, if they hear their colleagues talking about similar experiences in the past.*

Margaret: *And do you have any feedback, formal or informal, on these debriefs?*

Jules: *I think the informal feedback comes in quite a few ways, in that people generally now organise them and turn up to them and there isn't a reluctance to attend. Where you used to say, in the beginning of a debrief, 'Has anyone been to a debrief before?' only a few people would say they had. Now when you say, 'Has anyone NOT been to a debrief before?' most people have.*

So there's more of an opportunity to build resilience in staff in a debrief and to think about the future work, as opposed to just thinking back on a particular incident. So, informally, people just come back.

People stay often at the end and they might comment that it was useful, or a lot of people comment on how the sharing of certain information was so important for them. So people would say, 'I never knew that,' about either a part of the process, the incident, or about the person. People will often share bits of detail about the person who died, about their home life or a previous incident or something that had happened and that's a very important part. People will often pick up information that they didn't know, which they find very reassuring, which fits the puzzle to help them understand why this might have happened.

Margaret: *Yes.*

Jules: *They can make more sense of it, and people report being grateful for that bit of it. 'I've made more sense of it.' It's kind of a bit like the bomb shooting the team members all over the place; it also seems to have the effect that the understanding of the incident for each individual is shot all over the place. The debrief helps people to piece together a bit more of an understanding of why this particular person may have done what they did at that point of time.*

Margaret: *And then, making sense of something always reduces the trauma too.*

Jules: *Yes, and I suppose there's been the feedback on things like staff sickness and staff absence. Prior to this intervention, staff would go off sick after instances like this. Apparently people don't do that as much now.*

Margaret: *So there's some quite hard numbers that show that debrief model is extremely useful for the organisation, apart from its value to the individuals in the debrief?*

Jules: *Yes, and people say they value the fact that it's totally separate from the investigation and it's confidential and feels very much like it's a staff support meeting as opposed to any kind of information gathering, or people being under the spotlight, or ...*

Margaret: *It's really important, given that they're feeling so defensive about scrutiny, to make it a space in which they're not being scrutinised?*

Jules: *Yes.*

FOR REFLECTION

- Apart from debriefing, is there any time in an organisation you know in which a meeting for exchange of information and reflection is needed?
- How can team functioning be enhanced by such a meeting? What would the facilitator need to do to ensure this?

Last words

Human beings live and work in groups. We are primarily relational beings. Our groups are instrumental in our identity development and give us a sense of being supported as a person, as well as making available to us the ideas of others; diversities of human experience.

Convergent evidence from much research and also our own lived experience give a very clear picture of how those groups should be for the best experience, identity development and task achievement. Whether we are talking about families, nations, organisations, classrooms, clubs, teams or supervision/therapy groups, these are the principles of optimal functioning.

- Support should be maximised; blaming, criticism and negative interpretations should be minimised. Excessive anxiety should not be engendered.
- Leaders should be secure and not indulge in power plays, focusing principally on the welfare of group members, making space for their ideas and their individuality. They should see their task as enabling rather than controlling those they lead. Nevertheless, they must take on the responsibility of keeping to task. Their power should be

focused on maintaining good process, not on imposing their own ideas.

- When problems occur they should be confronted, not avoided. However, confrontation should be gentle and enquiring rather than condemning and aggressive. The support of individuals must be the over-riding principle. Good timing of confrontation is important; it should take place in a situation of minimal arousal.

- The culture should be optimised for admitting a diversity of ideas or even disagreements in a non-blaming milieu which maximises creativity. Difference can be celebrated, not seen as a threat.

- Participants' values and concordance of values underlie unity in diversity. Landscaping of values (Chapter 3) and deconstructing to illuminate personal and shared values (like the 'draw your coat of arms' exercise and the evoking of resonances) bring members into deeper alliance. Organisations, teams and other groups need to start with, and keep returning to, shared values.

- The facilitator has the responsibility of watching the process to ensure that the culture stays healthy and all voices can be heard. The facilitator might be the group leader but all members also have responsibility for the working of a group and the facilitative function might need to be with someone other than the leader.

Enjoy your groups! Choose them well, if possible. Noxious relationships ruin lives and undermine us all. Even for the sake of your career it might not be worth working in a dysfunctional team or organisation. But you have power to change as well as power to choose. Do keep a facilitator's mind-set and work constantly to improve the groups you live in. The more supportive your groups are, the clearer the communications, the better your chance of co-creating healthy identity development both for yourself and others. The more healthy your groups are, the better chance of achieving whatever tasks need to be accomplished.

I trust and pray that this book will give you the principles and some of the tools you need!

REFERENCES AND BIBLIOGRAPHY

Axelrod, R. H. (2000) *Terms of Engagement: Changing the Way We Change Organizations.* Berrett-Koehler Publishers, San Francisco, CA.

Barlow, S. H. (2013) *Speciality Competencies in Group Psychology.* Oxford University Press, New York.

Benard, B. (1991) *Fostering Resiliency in Kids: Protective Factors in the Family, School and Community.* National Resilience Resource Center, University of Minnesota, St Paul, MN.

Bion, W. (1961) *Experiences in Groups and Other Papers.* Tavistock Publications Ltd, London.

Brown, R. (2000) *Group Processes* (2nd edition). Blackwell Publishing, Oxford.

Bunker, B. B. & Alban, B. T. (1997) *Large Group Interventions: Engaging the Whole System for Rapid Change.* Jossey-Bass, San Francisco, CA.

Burck, C. & Daniel, G. (eds) (2010) *Mirrors and Reflections: Processes of Systemic Supervision.* Karnac Books, London.

Burtis, J. O. & Turman, P. D. (2006) *Group Communication Pitfalls.* Sage, Thousand Oaks, CA.

Byng-Hall, J. (1988) Scripts and legends in families and family therapy. *Family Process*, 27(2): 167–179.

Cooper, J. & Vetere, A. (2005) *Domestic Violence and Family Safety: A Systemic Approach to Working with Violence in Families.* Whurr/Wiley, London.

Davidovitz, R., Mikulincer, M., Shaver, P. R., Izsak, R. & Popper, M. (2007) Leaders as attachment figures: Leaders' attachment orientations predict leadership-related mental representations and followers' performance and mental health. *Journal of Personality and Social Psychology*, 93(4): 632–650.

Davies, G. M. & Dalgleish, T. (eds) (2001) *Recovered Memories: Seeking the Middle Ground.* Wiley, Chichester.

De Cremer, D., van Knippenberg, D., van Dijke, M. & Bos, A. E. R. (2006) Self-sacrificial leadership and follower self-esteem: When collective identification matters. *Group Dynamics: Theory, Research, and Practice*, 10(3): 233–245.

De Shazar, S. & Dolan, Y. (2007) *More than Miracles; The State of the Art of Solution-Focused Brief Therapy.* Haworth Press, Binghamton, NY.

Epston, D. & White, M. (1990) Consulting your consultants: The documentation of alternative knowledges. *Dulwich Centre Newsletter*, 4: 25–35. Republished 1992 in Epston, D. & White, M. *Experience, Contradiction, Narrative &*

Imagination: Selected papers of David Epston & Michael White, 1989–1991 (Chapter 1), pp. 11–26.

Eron, J. B. & Lund, T. W. (1996) *Narrative Solutions in Brief Therapy*. Guilford Press, New York.

Foulkes, S. H. & Anthony, E. J. (1957) *Group Psychotherapy: The Psycho-Analytic Approach*. Penguin Books, London.

Gantt, S. P. & Badenoch, B. (eds) (2013) *The Interpersonal Neurobiology of Group Psychotherapy and Group Process*. Karnac, London.

Haley, J. (1973) *Uncommon Therapy: The Psychiatric Techniques of Milton H Erickson MD*. Norton, New York.

Henning, M. (1992) Very brief family therapy in an African hospital. In Mason, J., Rubenstein, J. & Shuda, S. (eds). *From Diversity to Healing, papers from the 5th Biennial International Conference of the South African Institute of Marital and Family Therapy*, Durban.

Henning, M. (1995) The domain of the story. In *Old Ways, New Theories – Volume 1. Connect*. Zimbabwe Institute of Systemic Therapy, Harare.

Kottler, J. A. & Englar-Carlson, M. (2010) *Learning Group Leadership; An Experiential Approach*. Sage, Thousand Oaks, CA.

Lewis, C. S. (1952) *Mere Christianity*. Macmillan, New York.

Matsumoto, D., Frank, M. G. & Sung Hwang, H. (eds) (2013) *Nonverbal Communication: Science and Applications*. Sage, Thousand Oaks, CA.

McGoldrick, M., Gerson, R. & Shellenberger, S. (1999) *Genograms: Assessment and Intervention*. Norton, New York.

Mikulincer, M. & Shaver, P. R. (2007) Commentary: Attachment, group-related processes, and psychotherapy. *International Journal of Group Psychotherapy*, 57(2): 233–245.

Minuchin, S. (1974) *Families and Family Therapy*. Tavistock Publications, London.

Monk, G., Winslade, J., Crocket, K. & Epston, D. (eds) (1997) *Narrative Therapy in Practice: The Archaeology of Hope*. Jossey-Bass, San Francisco, CA.

Omer, H. (2004) *Non-violent Resistance: A New Approach to Violent and Self-Destructive Children*. Cambridge University Press, Cambridge.

Popper, M., Amit, K., Gal, R., Mishkal-Sinai, M. & Lisak, A. (2004) The capacity to lead: Major psychological differences between leaders and nonleaders. *Military Psychology*, 16(4): 245–263.

Rogers, C. R. (1995) *On Becoming a Person*. Houghton Mifflin, Boston, MA.

Seddon, J. (2014) *Report: Saving Money by Doing the Right Thing*. Locality/Vanguard, London.

Shaver, P. R. & Mikulincer, M. (2008) Augmenting the sense of security in Romantic, Leader-Follower, Therapeutic, and Group Relationships: a relational model of psychological change. In Forgas, J. & Fitness, J. (eds). *Social Relationships: Cognitive, Affective and Motivational Processes*. Psychology Press, Sydney.

Smith N. K., Cacioppo, J. T., Larsen, J. T. & Chartrand, T. L. (2003) May I have your attention, please: Electrocortical responses to positive and negative stimuli. *Neuropsychologia* 41: 171–183.

Thorne, B. & Sanders, P. (2013) *Carl Rogers (Key Figures in Counselling and Psychotherapy)*. Sage, London.

Vaughn, C. & Leff, J. P. (1985) *Expressed Emotion in Families: Its Significance for Mental Illness*. Guilford Press, New York.

Watzlawick, P., Baveas, J. B. & Jackson, D. D. (1967, 2011) *Pragmatics of Human Communication*. Norton, New York.

Weingarten, K. (1998) The small and the ordinary: The daily practice of a post-modern narrative therapy. *Family Process*, 37: 3–15.

White, M. (2007) *Maps of Narrative Practice*. W. W. Norton & Co, New York.

White, M. & Epston, D. (1990) *Narrative Means to Therapeutic Ends*. Norton, New York.

Whitely, J. S. & Gordon, J. (1979) *Group Approaches in Psychiatry*. Routledge and Kegan Paul, London.

Williams, M. & Penman, D. (2011) *Mindfulness: A Practical Guide to Finding Peace in a Frantic World*. Piatkus, London.

Yalom, I. D. & Leszcz, M. (2005) *The Theory and Practice of Group Psychotherapy* (5th edition). Basic Books, New York.

INDEX

Aggregate (not true group) 2, 17, 73
Aggression 11, 12, 18, 32, 79–80,
    102, 106–111, 124, 126
  dealing with 106–108, 126–127
  and other emotions 79–80,
    108–110
Alternative knowledges 5, 50–51,
    54–56, 69, 84, 86, 98, 139
Assumption of good faith 64–65,
    83, 87
Attachment 18–21, 35–39, 45, 49,
    73, 79, 100, 108, 110, 117, 139,
    140
  anxious 19, 20, 36–39, 73, 100, 108
  avoidant 19, 20, 36–39, 73, 79, 100
  and group process 35, 36, 37–39
  in leaders 18–20, 37–39
  own style 20–21, 36, 39
  mitigating effects of 20–21, 37–39
  secure 19, 20, 36–39, 100, 108,
    110, 117
  trauma 37, 52
Autonomic nervous system 107

Between-group difference 10
Between-group dynamics 10–11,
    25, 76
Body language 50
Bouncing the ball technique 83–84,
    93, 98, 105–106, 135

Catharsis 57–58, 67, 68, 85, 131
  extended 67
Causality 29, 31, 32, 96
  circular 29, 96
  linear 29, 31, 32

CBT (Cognitive Behaviour Therapy)
    2, 39, 54
Conflict 11–13, 29, 63, 99–102
  and confrontation 13
  and disagreement 12–13, 83,
    102, 111
  resolution 99–105
Confrontation 12–13, 21, 38, 73,
    104–110, 111, 138
Constructivism 47

Deconstruction 50–52, 56–57, 101,
    130, 138
Disagreement 12–13, 63–65, 83, 87,
    91, 93, 95, 96, 97–98, 102, 103,
    111, 138
  importance of 12, 83, 93, 95, 96,
    98, 111, 134, 138
Diversity 9, 15, 57, 66, 75, 86, 96,
    110, 111, 115, 117, 119–120, 121,
    124, 137, 138, 140
Dominant knowledge (story) 50–52,
    66, 69, 84, 87, 94, 110
Dragons in the undergrowth 76,
    88–89
Dropping hypothesis on the floor
    98
Dyadic conflict resolution 102–105
Dysfunctional (thin) story 6–7, 11,
    12, 30–31, 50–51, 52, 130

Eco map 39–42
Embodied memory 50
Empiricism 47–48
Empty chair technique 44
Encounter groups 2, 19

Escalation   11, 32, 79, 99, 100,
    101–102, 104
  complementary   101–102, 120
  countering   101–102, 104,
    108–109
  of conflict   11, 79, 100–102
  symmetrical   101–102, 120
Exceptions   52–54, 61, 69
Externalising   44, 54, 58–60, 69, 75,
    85, 103, 120

Fight or flight reaction   107

Genogram   33, 39–42, 140
Groups-
  cohesion   8, 10, 15, 22, 67, 76,
    80, 94
  constructed and natural   13–14,
    16, 23, 37, 45
  initiation   90
  internet   9, 10, 15–16
  open and closed   16, 70, 73, 90,
    114, 123–124
  relative permanence   14
  roles   1, 3, 4, 13, 18–19, 20, 21, 32,
    34–35, 42, 45, 80, 88, 91, 105,
    113, 132
  size   14–15, 70–71
Groupthink   82, 94–96

High Expressed Emotion (EE)   27,
    141

Idealism   47–48
Identified patient (IP)   27–28
Interdependence   73–74, 82
Internalised other interviewing
    44–45
Interrupting   105–106

Landscaping   54, 60–63, 138
  landscape of action
    (events)   61
  landscape of consciousness
    (values)   61, 138

Leadership   2–4, 8, 13, 14, 17, 18–21,
    22, 23, 34, 35, 39, 55, 64, 78,
    88–90, 94, 96, 101, 137–138, 139,
    140
  splits in   26–27
Locus of control   103

Meta-communication   50
Mindfulness   85, 141
Miracle question   3, 52, 53

Open and closed questions   55, 85
Outsider witnessing   55, 58, 66–67,
    69, 125–126, 130–131

Passive-aggression   96, 100, 106–111
Personal coat of arms   74, 86, 89, 138
Positivism   47, 49, 51–52
Power
  hierarchies   2, 4, 5, 7, 11, 26, 51,
    68, 80, 81, 87, 89, 91, 93, 94,
    96–98, 102, 106–107, 111, 113
  personal   8, 9, 17, 18, 43, 44, 59,
    95, 96–97, 98, 99, 109–110, 111,
    132, 137–138
Preferred future (outcome)   43–44,
    50, 53, 54, 55, 57, 61, 62, 65, 67,
    68, 69, 111
Problem plot (thin story)   50–51, 53,
    55, 62, 66, 69, 94, 105
Process   2, 6, 7, 9, 12, 17, 21, 23,
    29, 31, 32–33, 35, 36, 37, 39, 45,
    65, 68, 70, 74, 75, 81, 84, 90–97,
    101, 102, 103, 105, 106, 109, 113,
    116, 118, 119, 124, 126, 129, 130,
    132–133, 136, 138, 139, 140
  and attachment   35–39, 45
  as life habit   32–33, 36, 45, 101, 110
  commenting on   98, 104–105
  dyadic   30–31, 45
  inter-generational   33–34
  triadic   31–32, 45
  within-session   31, 32, 45, 53, 60,
    74, 75, 90, 94, 128, 132–133,
    138

Radical listening   56–57, 69, 82, 85, 87, 93, 95, 99, 100, 102, 106, 111
Rating scales   53
Realism   47
Re-membering   55, 66, 69

Scaffolding questions   54–55, 66–67
Scapegoating   1, 76, 104–105
Scripts, corrective and replicative   33–34, 42, 139
Sculpt   43–44
Secure base   37–38, 100, 110, 117
Silence/silencing
  and anxiety   3, 13, 85, 86, 87, 100

in Narrative work   55–56, 85–86, 98, 102, 105, 127, 130
Social constructionism   7, 47–50
Solution-focused therapy   48, 52–53, 54, 139
Subjective realities   22, 48, 57, 69, 94
Sympathetic nervous system   107
Systemic neutrality   30, 50–51

Transference and counter-transference   6, 30–31, 49

Utilisation   34–35, 88–89, 104

Within-group difference   10

Printed in Great Britain
by Amazon